The Only Earth We Know

Hymn Texts
by
Fred Kaan

*Joan Miller
with warmest greetings!*

Fred Kaan

Stainer & Bell/Hope

First published in 1999 by
Hope Publishing Company, Carol Stream, IL 60188, USA, and
Stainer & Bell Limited, PO Box 110, Victoria House, 23 Gruneisen Road,
London N3 1DZ, England.

British Library Cataloging-in-Publication Data
A catalogue record of this book is available from the British Library

ISBN: 0 85249 852 7 (World excluding USA and Canada)
ISBN: 0 916642 66 6 (USA and Canada)

Library of Congress Catalog Card No. 99-071815

Code No. 8064 (Hope Publishing Company)
Code No. B852 (Stainer & Bell Ltd)

Cover photograph courtesy of Pictor International

Printed in Great Britain by Galliards, Great Yarmouth, England.

Contents

Foreword

As long as there are people who know, and will tell, the story of hymnody in English in the second half of the twentieth century, Fred Kaan will have a place of special honour in that story.

He was, while minister of the Pilgrim Church in Plymouth in the 1960s, one of the pioneers of hymns in a modern idiom and hymns which speak of the city as well as the countryside. Moreover, with tenacious consistency from the first public appearance of *Pilgrim Praise* in 1968 to the present time, he has explored in his hymns the inner meanings of what the church says and does week by week, and has exposed the implications of its speech and practice for those who, both outside and inside its walls, exercise power and influence in society at every level. People who think that the Church has only its own business to mind (and they are all too many, Christian as well as non-Christian), tend to accuse Kaan of political partisanship because, like the eighth-century Hebrew prophets, he has a burning concern for social justice and global reconciliation, and because he will not stop challenging us to 'rise' and to 'risk' – two of the key words in this collection.

Fred does not wish this to be thought of as his definitive *oeuvre*. He is still very much working, and this book is a sort of milestone – an Eben-ezer, if you like: 'Hither by thy help I'm come,/And I hope...' Some may be surprised that so few of these texts strike the reader as overtly polemical. They are actually deeply peaceable, and the shock administered by the connections they make is only a shock to those whom Jeremiah derided, those who go on crying 'Peace! Peace!' where there is no peace, and ought not to be, until wrongs have been righted.

There are works here from every period of Kaan's output, with notes on the occasion which called each item into being. Ingenious in rhyme, and diverse in metre, these hymns make, on the page, a notable manual of modern devotion. Some have tunes to which they have become attached in popular use: one, the *Communion Calypso*, was written for its tune. Yet another, in its footnote, cries out for a tune to be written for it. Readers with access to hymn books containing a metrical index should have no difficulty in finding tunes suitable for most of them. Glad though we may be just to read them, Kaan's purpose in offering us his hymns is that they should be sung by congregations.

It is to be hoped that his critics, no less than his fans, will find themselves moved to gratitude by what is here. Certainly those who do not know, or hardly know, his work, are in for an enriching and renewing experience as they read and sing these pages.

Pocklington, York, England   Caryl Micklem
Spring 1999

Foreword

One of the most significant consequences of the British hymnic explosion of the 1960s and 1970s for American hymnody was its authors' reconstruction and restatement of the social gospel hymn. During this period, hymnal committees began to cast aside this genre because it featured an excessively optimistic appraisal of human endeavour to defeat systemic and surd evil. Local churches began singing reductionist-rhetoric peace-and-protest pop-style hymns from disposable supplements, which further challenged the style and message of classic social gospel hymns such as Frank Mason North's 'Where cross the crowded ways of life' (1905).

Just when it appeared that the future of hymns on social concerns might be determined by purveyors and consumers of a capricious pop culture, Erik Routley brought to the attention of US teachers, musicians, hymnal editors and publishers, including those involved with *Ecumenical Praise* (1977), hymns by Fred Kaan composed on a variety of social issues: these included world peace, reconciliation, liturgy and sacraments in a global and ecumenical setting, God's people gathered to be sent into the world as God's servant, and its people as pilgrims in a world in which the environment, as well as the human family, faced extinction.

I shall never forget an editorial meeting of the editors of *Ecumenical Praise* in the mid-1970s where Erik presented a copy of *Pilgrim Praise*. He had appropriately marked each page of the book with asterisks in three colours: red (must use), green (very important) and blue (perhaps). There were no pages without marks! Twelve of Fred's texts, more than those of any other writer, were included in this collection. Many of Fred's hymns have been set to a wide variety of music styles, and are included in recent hymnals; for example, eight in *The United Methodist Hymnal* (1989), ten in *The Presbyterian Hymnal* (1990), nine in *The Chalice Hymnal* (1995), four in *The New Century Hymnal* (1995), and nineteen in *Voices United* (1996).

Fred's hymns invariably have social justice at their centre. They are cries, laments and prophecies born in the church's struggle to be faithful to the gospel. Liturgical in origin and formation, and social in consequence, they intertwine biblical words and phrases of invitation, acceptance, risk-taking, vulnerability, freedom, and caring for each other, with memorable everyday phrases, such as 'Have your wits about us,' in *A hymn for the close of worship*, 'Until we know by heart the table of forgiveness,' in *A hymn on acceptance*, or 'Mary, Mary, quite contrary,' in *A tentative hymn to/about Mary*.

Puns and double meanings often bounce from the page, as in *A hymn for ex-centrics*. Fred's lines often shift from stressed to un-stressed rhythms, and mix heavy and lightweight metaphors and symbols. The latter exemplify what some experts, including composers, say hymn writers aren't supposed to do. As I read

Fred's recent work, it appears he still isn't bothered by this criticism – agreeing with it, in fact, whilst welcoming the notoriety.

I commend Fred's newest collection of hymns to readers and singers young and old, and applaud the publishers for making available this portrait of a preacher-pastor-scholar-poet's three-decade endeavour to make hymns and hymn-singing more biblical, catholic, celebrational, childlike, contextual, doctrinal, earthy, ecclesial, erudite, evangelical, exciting, humorous, imaginative, liturgical, mirthful, non-conforming, pastoral, political, prophetic, relevant, sensual, social, surprising, varied, vital, witty, and zestful!

Nashville, Tennessee, USA   Carlton R Young
Spring 1999   Editor, *The United Methodist Hymnal*

A note on the author

Fred Kaan was born in the Dutch city of Haarlem on 27 July 1929, the elder son of Herman Kaan, an employee of Netherlands Railways, and Brandina Kaan-Prinsen. Inclined politically to the left, his parents were only nominally religious, and from the time of his baptism in Haarlem's St Bavo cathedral until his late teens, Kaan scarcely set foot inside a church. Even so, the high-school tuition he received in religion, particularly from Hendrikus Berkhof, author of *Christ and the Powers* and later Professor of Dogmatics and Biblical Theology at Leiden University, intrigued him, and must have planted the seeds of his later vocation.

The Nazi occupation of Holland in 1940 changed Kaan's life dramatically, not only in terms of its resulting physical deprivations, symbolised especially by the 'hunger winter' of 1944/45 in which three of his grandparents perished, but also through the experience of his parents' involvement in the Dutch Resistance. For two years they sheltered a Jewish woman in their home, as well as a political prisoner who had escaped from Belsen. Emerging from the war a committed pacifist, Kaan joined the Netherlands Reformed Church in 1947. In 1949, abandoning plans to enter art school, he began the study of theology at Utrecht University. His move to Britain followed three years later when, inspired by reading Karl Barth, and encouraged through correspondence with an English pen-friend, he decided to offer himself for the ministry of the Congregational Union of England and Wales, a denomination which later merged with the Presbyterian Church of England and the Churches of Christ to become the United Reformed Church in the United Kingdom. Having entered the Western College, Bristol, Kaan graduated from Bristol University in 1954, and was ordained on 6 July 1955, being called to the ministry of the Windsor Road Congregational Church in Barry, South Wales.

If his experience so far had been largely that of study and preparation, the eight years Kaan spent at this church offered a changed agenda, one that involved him directly in the varied needs of a local congregation serving the community, and in particular, in the establishment of strong links with the international student movement in Britain. It was here, too, that he was first made aware of the importance of hymns to the Church's mission, an understanding that bore fruit after his appointment, in 1963, to the Pilgrim Church, Plymouth. Given freedom to explore untried forms of worship for his new and by its nature adventurous congregation, he began his hymn-writing career with the 50 texts gathered together in the words-only edition of *Pilgrim Praise*. They were written in response to a perceived lack of texts in the established hymnals, where the needs of Christian life and worship in a modern, urban setting seemed sadly neglected. First published privately, the contents of the collection were swiftly taken up by editorial committees worldwide, who found in them a freshness of theme and poetry that shed new insights into the working of Christ's gospel in contemporary society.

Kaan's appointment, in 1968, as Minister-Secretary of the International Congregational Council, London and Geneva, might have been seen as a potential distraction from his seminal role in what Erik Routley called the 'hymn explosion of the 1960s'. In fact, it was both the fulfilment of his growing commitment to the cause of internationalism (which had begun 'officially' in 1961, when he attended the Assembly of the International Congregational Council in Rotterdam), and the foundation of a fertile period of service to the Church that would inspire influential successors to *Pilgrim Praise* (1972), including *Break Not the Circle* (1975), *Songs and Hymns from Sweden* (1976), *The Hymn Texts of Fred Kaan* (1985) and *Planting Trees and Sowing Seeds* (1989). His texts have been translated into over 15 different languages. From 1969–74, he was a member of the editorial working group for the ecumenical and international hymnal *Cantate Domino*. Becoming an executive secretary of the newly formed World Alliance of Reformed Churches in 1970, Kaan for the next eight years undertook a hectic schedule of travel, with responsibilities that included involvement in the monitoring of human rights violations, aid projects, and communications. From 1971–72, he was text consultant for *New Songs of Asian Cities*. He was also editor of the four-language *Reformed Press Service*, managing editor of the quarterly journal *Reformed World*, and co-producer of the monthly radio programme *Intervox*, broadcast from the studio of the Ecumenical Centre in Geneva.

A decade of work based in Switzerland ended in 1978, with Kaan's appointment as Moderator of the West Midlands Province of the United Reformed Church in the UK. Characteristically refusing to renew this appointment in 1985, as a gesture against 'hierarchical thinking' within the Church, he subsequently became team minister of the Central (Ecumenical) Church, Swindon, and minister of Penhill United Reformed Church. A freelance translator and hymn-writer since 1989, Kaan has combined his busy life of travel and public speaking with the role of Secretary of the Churches' Human Rights Forum from 1993–97. Awarded an honorary Th.D from Debrecen Theological Academy, Hungary, in 1978, and a Ph.D (with distinction) from Geneva Theological College in 1984, he gained a certificate in counselling in 1989. He is a member of the Hymn Society in the United States and Canada, and the Hymn Society of Great Britain and Ireland.

The internationalism that has been so central to Kaan's ministry over the years has also characterised his family life. His first wife, Elly Steller (1928–93), was born in Indonesia of German and Dutch missionary parents. His elder son is married to a Swede; his younger son married a Hungarian and his daughter an Englishman. In 1994, after his first wife's death, he married Anthea Cooke, a medical doctor, whose first appointment was at a Church of South India hospital in Madras. Between them, the Kaans have a command of nine different languages (not counting Latin, Greek and Hebrew).

Nicholas Williams

About this book

Some time ago, a friend of mine who is the precentor at one of the more modern cathedrals in the land, sent me a letter in which he said:

> Do you by any chance have a complete collection of your hymns in their up-to-date versions? Every now and then I choose your hymns from *Ancient and Modern New Standard*, and wince slightly when I think you would probably have re-written them by now....

I wrote back to him to say that, no, I had not written a revised version of all my published texts, and I assured him that the slightness of his wincing did not in any way come close to the intensity with which I flinch at some of the things I had written – and at *how* I had written them – during the earlier phases of the past three decades or so.

The first practical thing I did was to produce a four-page errata slip entitled *The Hymn Texts of Fred Kaan – Suggested Changes*. Predictably, however, it proved to be somewhat ineffective in that, unlike a certain brand of Dutch lager, it failed to reach the parts that other.... Maybe that led to the point at which the idea was born that the publication of a collection of 'hymns already seen (but revised) and as yet unseen' might be a feasible project. I am grateful to my publishers, Stainer & Bell (UK) and Hope Publishing (USA) for responding positively to the idea, and for injecting the additional thought that it might be 'rather nice' to use the project to mark my 70th birthday.

My precentor-friend's suggestion of a complete collection of Kaan hymns in their up-to-date versions obviously was not on. His concern had clearly focused on the issue of sexist or non-inclusive language, especially people-of-God language. Some of the hymns incorporating this exclusive kind of terminology were manifestly capable of being revised; others, I felt, I could risk leaving unchanged; and then there were those that proved to be incorrigible and thus, at least for the time being, needed to be shelved in the basement.

Another factor militating against producing a complete collection (which would have meant publishing well over 200 titles) was the inevitable awareness that some texts had simply gone past their sell-by date, and needed to be put in a file downstairs, too.

In some way – though not entirely – this process of strict evaluation mirrors the way in which stringent criteria were applied in deciding whether a hymn should or should not be included in the hand-sized prototype edition of *Pilgrim Praise* in 1968. Whatever we then judged to be transitory material was quite firmly discarded, but in those days I tended not to keep any copies of rejects on file, not even for curiosity's sake.

The present serious trawl through my earlier books, together with a critical look at texts written since *Planting Trees and Sowing Seeds* came out in 1989, has resulted in this slimmed-down collection of one man's 100 hymns – give or 'take five' – for today and (I dare to hope) for some of our tomorrows. Those tomorrows will almost all be carved out of that hyped-up slice of time called the new Millennium. As the publication date of this book comes so close to the arrival of the year 2000, it was decided to place alongside the hymns the text of a cantata, *Magnificat for a New Millennium*, which the leading Norwegian composer Knut Nystedt and I were commissioned to write in connection with EXPO 2000, the World Exhibition in Hanover, Germany. The full score of this work is due to be published in Oslo by the Norwegian publishers Norsk Musikforlag roughly at the time that this hymn collection is coming out in Britain and the USA.

Although the cantata is not meant for congregational singing (it is set for mixed choir, four trombones and percussion), I do offer it here in the hope that it may serve as a text for personal devotional reading at this watershed time. You will discover that the opening words of the cantata also appear as a hymn in its own right – it is in fact the closing hymn in the book, with a textual change in verse 5, line 3. It is set there to a melody especially composed for it by Knut Nystedt; in the cantata itself these words are set to wholly different music, not in the style of a chorale or hymn.

You may wonder why the other hymn text in the cantata, 'Thank you, O God, for the time that is now', is also repeated in the corpus of the book. I felt that these words, too, should in their own right be incorporated in the hymn section under their original title of *The Present Tense*. The hymn dates from 1967 and was slightly revised in 1998.

Fifteen hymns in this collection are accompanied by full music especially composed for them by good friends of mine. In addition to Knut Nystedt (Norway), they are: Peter Churchill (UK) – 9; Maggie Hamilton (UK) – 84; Ron Klusmeier (Canada) – 44; the late Doreen Potter (Jamaica) – 3, 22 and 28; Pamela Ward (UK) – 41; and Carlton Young (USA) 1, 2, 25, 29, 32, 90 and 97. Their company in this collection is a source of delight and inspiration to me; I am deeply indebted to each and all of them.

Mind the Gap!

Little did I suspect at the time that my homespun hymn-writing at the Pilgrim Church in Plymouth (1963–68) would ignite one of the fuses that led to what Erik Routley called the 'hymn explosion' in the 1960s and 1970s (the other hymno-pyrotechnicians of course being Fred Pratt Green and Brian Wren).

Unlike some of my fellow hymn-writers, I never had on my agenda the idea of wanting to write hymns; it wasn't and still isn't a matter of ambition. I still say to groups of people who invite me to talk about my work after all these years that I am the most surprised hymn-writer in the world. I started writing because I had to. No, let me rephrase that: because *we together*, as a worshipping and outreaching congregation, were confronted Sunday by Sunday with the *lacunae*, the inadequacies, the heaven-focused unserviceability of much that was on offer in our previous-generation hymn book, *Congregational Praise* (1951), which was by any standards a good hymnal, ahead of its time.... I *had* to.

'Tell me what you sing, and I'll tell you who you are', said Albert van den Heuvel. I felt – we felt – that much of what we sang routinely said little or nothing about who we were and what made us tick, about how we saw our role as ministers of reconciliation in the world and as replenishers of the earth. We had our doubts about the extent to which our hymn-singing echoed, let alone strengthened, the 'groaning of creation'.

Van den Heuvel in the mid-sixties warned that 'our unrenewed hymn book is a greater obstacle to the renewal of our churches than all our outdated theological utterances.' He acknowledged there are hymns that were written once and for all but that

> ...traditional hymns can only live when new ones are also sung. Since singing is a dynamic activity in which a community expresses itself, it must be a combination of both. Therefore new hymns are as important as old ones. And the old ones have to be continually tested, theologically, musically and poetically. Unauthentic language or simply bad music corrupts our faith. They give both the outsider and the participant the wrong concept of God.

Much has been newly written and composed since then. After an interim period during which paperback supplements in proliferation lived side by side with previous-generation hymnals, churches all over the world have by now published their new hard-cover hymn books, most of which look refreshingly different from their preceding editions, though it also needs to be said that in a minority of cases 'new' hymn books are sad examples of restoration rather than of renewal. Yet we can only truly sing in church if we are really connected with the *dynamic* principle of tradition and of 'remembering forward'. In my introduction to Alan Gaunt's excellent new collection of hymns, *Always from Joy* (Stainer & Bell, 1997), I have described the high quality of his book 'as a critique – by inference – on much of what passes for "modern" in the worship life of many a congregation: the junk-food choruses, soundbite songs, imitation mantras set to trite music'.

My good friend Carlton (Sam) Young, composer, theologian and irrepressible wit, of Nashville, Tennessee, once came to a hymn-related event in London, and as he entered the foyer of the hotel where the meeting was taking place, he was hooting with laughter. He had just come out of Charing Cross underground station where – when he got off the train – he heard a sepulchral voice saying repeatedly: 'Mind the gap!' And Sam said to us: 'At first I had no idea what it was all about and for whom it was meant, but then the thought occurred to me that this was the public announcement of a new theology.' He then elaborated: mind the gap between what happens in church and what needs to be done after the blessing; mind the gap between receiving the broken bread at the table/altar and breaking bread with the world's hungry.

A mind-the-gap theology! Is there not a parallel need for a mind-the-gap hymnody? Is it not a prime responsibility for those of us who are trying to write hymns for today and tomorrow to acknowledge the gap between word (Word) and deed, worship and mission, liturgy and involvement; between prayer and doing our damnedest to make that prayer come true? Because, after all, as we cannot fail to have noticed, there are things God will *not* do for us, and here I think that the theology of the 'old-fashioned' Sunday school hymn by Susan Warner (1819–85), 'Jesus bids *us* shine with a pure clear light, like a little candle burning in the night', is a great deal closer to an incarnational understanding of our calling to be Christ's witnesses and servants in the world than praying 'Shine, Jesus, shine'. 'The work that Christ *began* to do we humbly pledge ourselves to share', as I put it in the first hymn I ever wrote – a post-communion hymn! (See *Acts* 1:1, Authorized Version.)

In Micah's vision of the Kingdom, of peace/shalom, there is talk of people beating swords into ploughshares, *not* praying them into ploughshares! Beating, hammering, is hard work, requiring energy.

It is part of the human covenanted mandate that there are things only *we* can do, rather than that we should sit down with our hands serenely folded in the hope that God will intervene 'from above':

> Give to your people confidence in striving
> for life that is in faith and act complete;
> redeem us from the blasphemy of praying
> with lazy hands and unintending feet. (7)

When Isaac Watts, writing about the amazing, divine love of a totally self-giving Christ, sang that 'it demands my soul, my life, my all', he was saying that there is no such thing as non-committal hymn-singing, no worship without strings attached. Erik Routley, for whom praise was a 'duty and delight', has an equally demanding line in one of the finest hymns he ever wrote:

> in praise is earth transfigured by the sound
> and sight of heaven's everlasting feast.

True or false? Is that how the average congregation sees praise and worship? As a means of transfiguring, transforming, changing, saving the earth? What *is* the logical outcome of our hymn-singing? Does there *have* to be a consequence to what we do (do?) in church? I know that for some people worship in church stands on its own, in isolation. It is a private affair ('I in my Saviour am happy and blest'), which incorporates their belief in what Margaret Thatcher once said, that 'there is no such thing as society'; so life can be compartmentalised, and there is no such thing either as the implementation or application or making-real of the Gospel. But the fallacy of this trend of thought is that the only place where there is no society is that minute island on which you are cast away alone, without back-references such as books or CDs, and with no hope of coming face to face, or 'eyeball to eyeball', with another human being created in the image of God.

Eyeball to eyeball is a helpful phrase to remind us that when we look another person in the eye, we see a tiny mirrored image of our selves. It is in the pupil of the Other's eye that I see the 'pupilla' (Latin: little doll) – reflection of my Self. The transfiguration/transformation of the earth and society flows logically from the duty and delight of coming face to face with God in worship.

The most impressive church I ever preached in was in Kiribati in the Central Pacific – the building consisted of no more than a straw roof supported by a dozen or so wooden posts. All around us, there was the village, the world, the living-together of people. A society visible and audible from 'within' the church; the smell of cooking on woodfires wafting into the congregation like a descant to our hymn-singing. A church without walls! If only the climate in Birmingham were different, I sometimes think...

The Only Earth We Know

So, what about the title of this book? Two of the texts in it end with these words – the only earth we know. One is the very first hymn in the book, taken from a cantata commissioned by 'Save the Children' in the Nordic countries, and premiered in 14 different Scandinavian cities on the same day at the same time in 1995. The last descriptive verse says:

> The scene: imagination is a tree,
> its roots in-earthed, its branches reaching out.
> Imagine life as it is meant to be!
> Make people whole, bring peace on earth about!
> The scene is set, above, below;
> this is the only earth we know. (1)

The other text is less earth-wide, and more on an intimate scale. I wrote it for the memorial service of a close friend who died too soon of cancer at the age of 56. The hymn, which is entitled *A Hymn of Grateful Recall and Renewed Commitment*, and which contains the recurring reference to a 'God who came and comes', ends with these words:

> Then leave us God, who comes and goes,
> in human-ness to grow,
> to care for people, tend the earth:
> – the only earth we know! (66)

Whatever the scale, inter-national or inter-personal, the context in which human life is played out is that of the earth and of the here-and-now: we know no other scenario.

As I cast my mind back over more than three decades of hymn-writing, and reread what I wrote to introduce *The Hymn Texts of Fred Kaan*, fourteen years ago, I will confess that any biblical detective work, any dissection of systematic theology, any hymnic DIY, or the sheer delight at being alive on this earth at this time, keeps steering me as irresistibly now as then towards a passionate commitment to let the doctrines of creation and of God-becoming-human, like us, be the only relevant co-ordinates on the map of my life. If God lovingly and deliberately created this earth, and came to earth not in theory but in flesh-and-blood reality, then *this* earth and *this* humanity (ours and Christ's) matter infinitely: 'what God has joined together, let no one put asunder.'

The editorial board of *Genesis* 1 fails to say so, but the book of *Job* tells us that the act of creation, that transfiguration from chaos to peace-and-order was set to cosmic song by stars and angels. At the transfiguration of an invisible God into a visible, physical Christ, a whole choir of angels was brought on to sing 'Glory to God in the highest and on *earth* peace....' Like the creation, the incarnation was/is a physical down-to-earth event, and glory to God in the highest is tightly interwoven with there being peace on earth. In a seemingly disconnected story – that of Palm Sunday – we are told (provided you read it as Luke describes the event, which differs from the way the other gospel writers saw it), that it was not the Jerusalem crowd, the general public, but Jesus's own disciples who staged his entry into the city: the whole company of his disciples began to sing aloud, hosanna and all that, but then... 'Peace in heaven'. Hadn't they learnt anything during the three years they spent in his company? I find the whole thing quite bizarre: the angels (whatever angels – and heaven! – may be) sang 'Peace on earth' when a child was born, but the disciples sang 'Peace in heaven' when a man was about to be tortured to death. Peace in heaven is none of our business, because the glory of God has a direct bearing on the here-and-now where Christ is present (!) and it is in the everyday setting of our earthy world and human society that we are called to practise what we sing. Peace on earth *is* our business, and I do believe that the transfiguration of the earth does begin in praise; but the implication is that our churches should 'have no walls'...

The Jamaican composer Doreen Potter (1925–80) with whom I worked very closely during my Geneva days – particularly in the production of a small book of hymns, *Break Not the Circle*, which was launched at the 1975 Nairobi Assembly of the World Council of Churches (and which is still available from Stainer & Bell) – occasionally wrote a text as well, one of which became very popular at the WCC Vancouver Assembly three years after her untimely death.

The verses of the hymn pose the question, in varied forms: Jesus, where can we find you in our world today? The refrain then suggests the answer and the challenge:

> Look at your brother beside you;
> look at your sister beside you.
> Look! Listen! Care!

It may also be a good idea to have another look at *Matthew* 25: 31–46, and to keep looking – while singing – being and doing!

Birmingham, England   Fred Kaan
Easter 1999

Magnificat for a New Millennium

Come! Sing and live a world Magnificat,
the new Millennium with hope embrace.
Now is the time for trust and taking sides:
say 'yes' in love to all the human race.

Reach out in faith to what is still unknown,
each day a first day, every dawn a birth,
new ground for sowing seeds and planting trees,
'Lest we forget' the future of the earth.

Praise all that makes the world a better place:
creative thought, invention and design,
the anvil and the plough of making peace,
of sharing land and shelter, bread and wine.

Risk to become all we are meant to be,
live out tomorrow's destiny today!
Let us unite to keep the dream alive:
a world at peace, the human race at play.

As past and future in the present meet
and we take stock of where we were and are,
may confidence inspire our forward way,
and love with justice be our guiding star.

Come! Sing and live a world Magnificat
for water, soil and air – the mystic trinity
of all that is today, of all that came to be,
created, sent evolving from the void of chaos
to the order of the day...

Water

water, giving rise to life, to earth, to birth,
cleansing water, quenching thirst,
streams of water, new beginnings.
Still water – as in lake – yet never still,
cascading from eternity to here;
heart-beating surf, pulsating moon-drawn sway
from oceans' farthest shore
to where you are, I am, with all the world...

Cry 'Kyrie' for pride and greed
in poisoned rivers manifest,
for waters, wasted unto death,
for streams imprisoned by prestigious dams;
for dying-crying seas
and oceans giving rise
to children's lives de-formed;
for mines and missiles poised
amid the grave of fish:

Kyrie eleison, Kyrie eleison, Kyrie eleison.

Come! Sing and live a world Magnificat
for water, soil and air – the mystic trinity
of all that is today, of all that came to be,
created, sent evolving from the void of chaos
to the order of the day...

Soil

earth-womb, shielding-yielding hope (world without end!)
cradling ore and food for life,
scene of quest and exploration:
atomic power, the alphabet, the wheel,
technology and healing, music, art.
This island earth, one home for humankind,
where rights and tasks are shared
like bread and wine, enough for everyone...

Cry 'Kyrie' for pride and greed:
the politics of selfish gain,
oppressing those without a voice;
abuse of skills, inventiveness and power.
Cry for the death of trees,
research seduced for ill,
to cripple and to kill;
for arms refined and aimed
at ending life and birth:

Kyrie eleison, Kyrie eleison, Kyrie eleison.

Come! Sing and live a world Magnificat
for water, soil and air – the mystic trinity
of all that is today, of all that came to be,
created, sent evolving from the void of chaos
to the order of the day...

Air

oxygen, sustaining life, food for the heart,
air for breathing, yet unbound,
air pronouncing birds and fragrance,
day's backcloth for the dialogue of souls,
blue playing-field for vapour trails and clouds,
for longings taking flight to see the world,
where love awaits, work is,
feet walk on air in freedom and delight...

Cry 'Kyrie' for pride and greed,
the shredding of the atmosphere
and lead that lines our city streets;
our peaceful valleys torn by screams of war -
dark bombers in the skies.
Shed tears for acrid smoke,
dioxin down the road,
as acid drizzle falls
on radioactive grass:

Kyrie eleison, Kyrie eleison, Kyrie eleison.

Come! Sing and live a world Magnificat
for water, soil and air – the mystic trinity
of all that is today, of all that came to be,
created, sent evolving from the void of chaos
to the order of the day...

So let every town and city,
every hamlet, every home
humbly, strongly meet the challenge
of the new Millennium.

Let us bless the world around us
in our ways of thought and speech,
by our actions, our awareness,
of the needs of all and each.

Reaching out to others, let us
vow to heal the hurt of earth,
seek the welfare of the nations,
human dignity and worth:

And now my friends: all that is true,
all that is noble, all that is just and pure,
all that is loveable and attractive,
whatever is excellent and admirable –
fill your thoughts with these things...
and always be thankful!

Philippians 4:8...*Colossians* 3:15

The Present Tense

Thank you, O God, for the time that is now,
for all the newness your minutes allow,
make us alert with your presence of mind
to fears and longings that move humankind.

Thank you, O God, for the time that is past,
for all the values and thoughts that will last.
May we all stagnant tradition ignore,
leaving behind things that matter no more.

Thank you for hopes of the day that will come,
for all the change that will happen in time;
God, for the future our spirits prepare,
hallow our doubts and redeem us from fear.

Make us afraid of the thoughts that delay,
faithful in all the affairs of today;
keep us, Creator, from playing it safe,
thank you that now is the time of our life!

Fred Kaan

The Only Earth We Know

Hymn Texts
by
Fred Kaan

*To my friends without number
all over the world
who throughout my life
have welcomed me into their home
and broken their bread with me
who have accepted me as I am
with whom I have shared tears and laughter
whose wit and wisdom have enriched me
whose faith and doubt have challenged me
whose warmth of human-ness has affirmed
my delight at being an earthling
I dedicate this book:*

Love and Peace!

1 In the beginning: God!

1 Imagination is a tree 10.10.10.10.8 8.

Before all time, love's logic spoke the Word
that from unordered water, chaos, night,
brought to the fore – wherever it was heard –
the miracle of ordered space and light.
    The scene is set for life and love:
    earth underfoot, the sky above.

With time in place, into the womb of earth
love sowed the seeds of all that came to be,
a world of hope and never-ending birth;
(and at the heart of all there stands a tree!)
    The scene is set for life and love:
    earth underfoot, the sky above.

That tree! Among its leaves the birds shall nest
and children come and shelter in its shade.
The scene is set for somersault and feast,
to celebrate the move love's logic made.
    The scene is set for life and love:
    sky underfoot, the earth above!

The scene: imagination is a tree,
its roots in-earthed, its branches reaching out.
Imagine life as it is meant to be!
Make people whole, bring peace on earth about!
    The scene is set, above, below;
    this is the only earth we know.

Fred Kaan

In 1995 I was commissioned, in collaboration with the leading Norwegian composer Knut
Nystedt, to write the text of a cantata to mark the 75th anniversary of 'Save the Children' in
the Nordic countries. The work was premiered on the same day and at the same time in 14
cities in Denmark, Iceland, Norway and Sweden. Trigger for the work, *One mighty
flowering tree*, was a quotation by Black Elk, a Holy Man of the Oglala Sioux, describing a
vision he had had when nine years old: 'And I saw all things in the spirit ... and I saw in the
centre growing one mighty flowering tree to shelter all the children. And I saw that it was
holy.'
Suggested tune: EARTH SONG

EARTH SONG

Music Carlton R Young (1926–)
Words Fred Kaan (1929–)

𝅗𝅥. = 58

Be - fore all time, love's log - ic spoke the
to the fore wher - ev - er it was

Word___ that from un-or-dered wa - ter, cha - os, night,___ brought
heard___ the mi - ra - cle of or-dered space and

light.___ The scene is set for life and love:

earth un-der-foot, the sky___ a - bove.___

slow arpeggios,
sustaining pedal on

know.___

2 A time-warp hymn

6.4.6.4.6 4.

Before a Word was said,
God had our ear;
before the world was made,
Jesus was here.
Ahead of Abraham,
God was, I am.

Before the Word assumed
our flesh and blood,
Jesus among us roomed
and with us stood.
Ahead of Abraham,
God was, I am.

God, Span of future, past,
our present Tense,
your Word is first and last:
eternal Sense.
Ahead of Abraham,
you are – I am.

Fred Kaan

Written for Central (Ecumenical) Church, Swindon, in 1987, in connection with a series of worship services focused on the I AM sayings of Jesus. The words 'Before Abraham was, I am' (*John* 8:58) have always particularly fascinated me. Could it be that 'the present tense' (see No. 53), and the 'here-and-now', deserve more emphasis and commitment?

Suggested tune: TIME-WARP

TIME-WARP

♩ = 92–100

Music Carlton R Young (1926–)
Words Fred Kaan (1929–)

Be-fore a Word was said,

God had our ear; be - fore the world was made,

Je - sus was here. *ten.* A-head of A - bra-ham,

1–2 *rall.* *reflective*   **3** *reflective*

God was, I am. you are – I am – you are.

3 A hymn of first, last and in-between

6.6.6.6.D.

In the beginning: God!
No earth or sea or skies.
In the beginning: God,
but nothing other-wise.
In the beginning: Word,
unheard and still unseen;
not even brooding bird,
no space or time for scene.

When all is said and done
(in the beginning: God!),
when earth has been and gone,
there will be only God,
who is the first and last,
the seed and sum of life;
there will be no more thirst,
no crying, pain or death.

But for the great between,
unending, unbegun,
the things that can't be seen
are named and they are done.
God gives the human race
its likelihood divine,
its hours and ways of space,
its alphabet of time.

The great between is now
and time is ours to tell.
God comes and shows us how
to stand and walk and spell.
So life becomes a feast,
a round to set us free,
for God is first and last
and in between are we!

Fred Kaan

I wrote this text in 1974 when I was involved in the production of a radio programme in Geneva, commemorating Duke Ellington, who had died shortly before. Among the Duke's formidable creative output, his Sacred Concerts stand out in particular for me. I shall never forget how moved I was when I heard his jubilant and witty treatment of 'In the beginning: God'. The tune Doreen Potter wrote for this hymn I judge to be the finest she ever composed.

Suggested tune: KANELLI

KANELLI

Music Doreen Potter (1925–80)
Words Fred Kaan (1929–)

In the be-gin-ning: God! No earth or___ sea or skies. In the_ be-gin-ning: God, but noth-ing oth-er -wise. In the be-gin - ning: Word,___ un-heard and still_ un-seen;___ not e-ven brood - ing bird, no space or__ time for__ scene.___

4 The first and final word

8.7.8.7.8.7.

God who spoke in the beginning,
forming rock and shaping spar,
set all life and growth in motion,
earthly world and distant star;
God who calls the earth to order
is the ground of what we are.

God who spoke through people, nations,
through events long past and gone,
showing still today love's purpose,
speaks supremely through the Son;
God who calls the earth to order
speaks the Word and it is done.

God whose speech becomes incarnate
– Christ is Servant, Christ is Lord –
calls us to a life of service:
heart and will to action stirred.
God who uses our obedience
has the first and final word.

Fred Kaan

Much as I value *good* contemporary translations of the bible, I do regret the inevitable disappearance of a phrase frequently occurring in the Authorized Version: 'and it came to pass that...' Whenever God speaks, things happen; think of the Word becoming earth, 'body of God'; think of the Word becoming a human being!

Suggested tune: CORBRIDGE

5 We must evolve it

5.5.5.4.5 5 5.4.

God the narrator,
logically speaking,
in the beginning
shaped the good earth.
   Out of this true love
   speaking-and-do-love
   blossomed and grew love:
   life came to birth.

God-the-beginning
spoke and created
life in its fullness:
people alive.
   Born to subdue-love,
   care-and-pursue-love,
   make-and-speak-true-love,
   born to survive.

This is the sequel
of the narration:
we must evolve it
to the good end,
   drawing on do-love,
   every-day-new-love,
   seeing-it-through-love
   peace to extend.

Fred Kaan

This text, written in 1972, was triggered off by the awareness that in Hebrew there is only one word for 'word' and 'deed', and that the opening line of John's Gospel about the Word (*logos*) being there from the beginning has logical (!) consequences – for *us*. To quote *James* 1:22: we must be 'doers of the word'. This gives us an earth-bound ministry.

Suggested tune: BUNESSAN

6 God in the midst

6.6.6.6.8 8.

God is unique and one –
Maker, Sustainer, Lord!
Patterns of life were spun
by his creative Word.
  Of his intention, love and care
  we are with growing trust aware.

Love came to earth in Christ,
our common life to share,
choosing to be the least,
willing a cross to bear.
  He died and rose, that we might live
  and all our love – responding – give.

The Holy Spirit moves
people to trace God's plan;
such inspiration proves
more than the mind can span.
  Each listening heart is led to find
  the will of God for humankind.

God shall forever reign,
Ruler of time and space;
here, in the midst of life,
seen in the human face.
  We give expression to our creed
  by love in thought and word and deed.

Fred Kaan

This is an attempt at writing a credal hymn, for which I had Martin Shaw's tune LITTLE
CORNARD in mind. I wrote it for the Pilgrim Church in Plymouth in 1968.
Suggested tune: LITTLE CORNARD

7 A hymn for growing Christians 11.10.11.10.

Great God, who on the Friday of creation
conferred on us the freedom of the earth,
help us to make the most of all the choices
you set before us at the dawn of birth.

Give to your people confidence in striving
for life that is in faith and act complete;
redeem us from the blasphemy of praying
with lazy hands and unintending feet.

We long to *be*! – so draw our will to Jesus
whose cross is planted on the day we're born;
then help us to accept a life of Fridays,
to call them good, and live on love alone.

God, give us grace to honour you by choosing
the risk of growing up and taking care;
teach us, while wholly on your strength depending,
to live our life *as if* you were not there.*

Fred Kaan

*so to speak!

I wrote this text during the 1983 residential conference of Provincial Moderators of the United Reformed Church. I do not know why, but it occurred to me that in the Genesis 'week' about the creation, man/woman were made on the day before the Sabbath, and that the crucifixion also happened on a Friday ... 'Living a life of Fridays' therefore implies new beginnings and a call to remember Christ's self-sacrifice.

Suggested tune: ZU MEINEM HERRN

As the glory of creation
and the thrill of human love,
as the wonder at a cradle,
at the things that live and move,
  higher still, uncaught in word,
  is the glory of the Lord.

As the glory of a concert
and the skill of those who play,
as the joy of book and painting,
shapes in stone and bronze and clay,
  higher still, uncaught in word,
  is the glory of the Lord.

As the glory of the future
and the teaching of the past,
as the challenge of the present
and the here-and-now of Christ,
  higher still, uncaught in word,
  is the glory of the Lord.

In the life and work of Jesus,
in his dying on a cross,
in the great surprise of Easter
giving people gain for loss,
  here we catch and taste the Word
  spelling glory to the Lord!

Fred Kaan

This hymn was written during the Centenary Consultation of the World Alliance of Reformed Churches in St Andrews, Scotland, in 1977. Theme of the event was: 'The glory of God and the future of man' (today we would probably say 'future of humanity').

Suggested tune: ALL SAINTS

2 We shall find Christ among us

Advent (including Mary)
Christmas
Lent and Passion Sunday
Holy Week and Easter
Post-Easter
'Ascension'

9 A tentative hymn to/about Mary

with asterisks (stardust)

8.7.8.7.

STARDUST

Music Peter Churchill (1963–)
Words Fred Kaan (1929–)

Ma - ry, Ma - ry, quite con - tra - ry, re - bel,

(Bass) Ma - ry, Ma - ry, re - bel,

giv - ing ear to God, earth - sop - ra - no, sing - ing

etc.

free - dom: Zi - on's song — in 'yes' — and blood;

Mary, Mary, quite contrary,
rebel, giving ear to God,
earth-soprano*, singing freedom:
Zion's song in 'yes' and blood;

earmarked Mary, world-affirming,
in compliance giving birth,
your defiance** gave us Jesus,
Word-among-us, run to earth.

Mary, mouthpiece of God's people***,
Sister Chosen, giving voice,
Ave Mary****, Eve of Easter,
Bibi Maryam*****, Sister Choice;

Mary/Miriam******, ever-bearing
life as hope for all to share,
make us, women, men and children
as expectant as you are!

Fred Kaan

Stardust

* Soprano comes from the same root as sovereign (sovrano – Italian), and has something to do with being high or supreme. Some traditions call Mary 'Queen of Heaven'. She is in a sense 'prima donna', first lady – yet, as in a choir, she is first among equals; it takes contralto, tenor and bass to complete the whole. All the choir is (God-)parent to Jesus, who is the Child of humanity.

** Mary wasn't just a compliant woman whom we often tend to glamorise by turning her into a somewhat ethereal figure, tall, slim and blonde, like a Swedish filmstar, dressed in immaculate (!) blue – Presbyterian blue – on a plinth in a niche with suitable back-lighting. Her acceptance of her role was very much an act of defiance: what will the neighbours have said, or the elders at the synagogue?

*** The Magnificat isn't exclusively Mary's own work. If there had been some Zealot copyright lawyer around at the time, he could have taken her to court for committing plagiarism. Almost all her song is quotation from the Old Testament. She makes herself a mouthpiece of the whole people of God; she becomes that 'daughter of Zion' (see verse 1, line 4). There are only two original lines in the Magnificat: 'My soul magnifies the Lord' (*Luke* 1: 46) and 'henceforth all generations shall call me blessed' (vs 48).
J. S. Bach with his uncanny sensitivity to the secondary layers of the bible, seems to have rumbled verse 48. In his version of the Magnificat he has the choir sing 'omnes generationes' (all generations) no less than 96 times! Mary's *own* words, as distinct from those she recalls and quotes, are future-orientated – she 'remembers forward'. How could it be other-wise? She was pregnant, for God's sake!

**** Ave Maria (Hail Mary). Read Ave backwards and you get Eva, which is how most European languages spell Eve ... but of course, eve is also the forerunner of the coming dawn.

***** Maryam (a two-syllable word, with the y pronounced as in year) is the name whereby Mary is known among Muslims. Bibi is a term of veneration used for women saints and prophets.

****** Mary in Hebrew is Miriam, meaning 'the rebellious one' (see verse 1, lines 1 and 2). Moses' sister Miriam led the women in a triumphant song-and-dance routine after Israel's liberating trek through the Red Sea (see verse 1, line 3).

In 1994 I was invited to write a Hymn to Mary for a local ecumenical hymnbook supplement. My first reaction was: 'What! Me? One of Calvin's boys?' Then I thought again ... and this is the result. The hymn should always be printed with the (rather elaborate) footnotes, or asterisks (diminutive for stars). I thought that stardust might be an appropriate word to bring in to ensure a 'Christmassy mood'. Peter Churchill wrote a wonderfully witty tune for it.

Suggested tune: STARDUST

Tomorrow Christ is coming
as yesterday he came;
a child is born this moment
– we do not know its name.
The world is full of darkness,
again there is no room;
the symbols of existence
are stable, cross and tomb.

Tomorrow will be Christmas,
the feast of love divine,
but for the nameless millions
the star will never shine.
Still is the census taken
with people on the move;
new infants born in stables
are crying out for love.

There will be no tomorrows
for many a baby born.
Good Friday falls on Christmas
when life is sown as corn.
But Jesus Christ is risen
and comes again in bread
to still our deepest hunger
and raise us from the dead.

Our God becomes incarnate
in every human birth.
Created in God's image,
we *must* make peace on earth.
God will fulfil Love's purpose
and this shall be the sign:
we shall find Christ among us
as woman, child or man.

Fred Kaan

Written for Advent 1966, and submitted to Southern Television in a 'Hymn for Britain'
contest. The hymn is all about today and tomorrow, about the 'real presence' of Christ (and I
am not talking about a liturgical/doctrinal concept....!)

Suggested tune: CRUGER

11   A hymn of homelessness

10 10.10 10.

Each year we sing with bated Christmas voice
as if events in Bethlehem were nice;
when every house and pub had shut its door
and Mary in a shed her baby bore.

Forgive us, God, that things are still the same,
that Christ is homeless under other names;
still holy fam'lies to our cities come
where life is sick and sore in crowded slum.

God, make it clear that joy will be denied
unless the door into our life stands wide;
that even with our tables richly spread
our house of life is short of living bread.

Give to your people restlessness of soul
till right is done and life is healed and whole;
keep us impatient till the time has come
when all your children are on earth at home.

Fred Kaan

Originally called 'A hymn for Shelter', this text was written for the Housing Action Group
Shelter, when I was closely involved in the formation of the Plymouth branch of that
organisation in 1965.

Suggested tune: FARLEY CASTLE

12 An uneasy carol

11.10.11.10.

We come uneasy, God, this festive season,
afraid that all may be just as before;
so hallow, help us use, each restive reason
that makes us want to see through tale and lore.

We come uneasy, longing to be able
to look beyond the symbols and the signs,
to find behind our carols and the bible
the living Word, as read between the lines.

We come uneasy, asking for your leading
to take our distance from the manger-scene
and go into our mainstreets for our reading
of all that can in people's eyes be seen.

We come, uneasy at the thought of knowing
the child who suffers, all who die too soon:
you, earthy-Christ, in human likeness growing
from cradle of the night to cross at noon.

We welcome you, uneasy at your coming,
but reassured that you have come to stay
to bind together your and our becoming
a sign of hope, a light to save the day.

Then free us from traditions that diminish
the glory of your Christmas to a farce;
make good our will, from yearly start to finish
to 'see this thing that (daily!) comes to pass'.

Fred Kaan

© 1981 Hope Publishing Company for USA and Canada and Stainer & Bell Ltd for all other territories

This hymn owes its origin to what three of 'my' ministers (I was at the time Moderator of the West Midlands Province of the United Reformed Church) wrote in their church magazines in Advent 1980. I owe them a debt of gratitude. What concerns me so deeply is not just the commercial hijacking of Christmas, but the appalling lack of imagination and style with which so many churches seem to go through the motions in celebrating the incarnation.

Suggested tune: INTERCESSOR or CITY OF GOD

13 The tree springs to life   5.5.5.5.6.5.6.5. or 10 10.11 11.

We meet you, O Christ,
in many a guise;
your image we see
in simple and wise.
You live in a palace,
exist in a shack.
We see you, the gardener,
a tree on your back.

In millions alive,
away and abroad,
involved in our life,
you live down the road.
Imprisoned in systems,
you long to be free.
We witness you, Jesus,
still bearing your tree.

We hear you, O Man,*
in agony cry.
For freedom you march,
in riots you die.
Your face in the papers
we read and we see.
The tree must be planted
by human decree.

You choose to be made
at one with the earth;
the dark of the grave
prepares for your birth.
Your death is your rising,
creative your word:
the tree springs to life
and our hope is restored!

Fred Kaan

* or Christ

I wrote this for a BBC television programme I did on Passion Sunday 1966, which happened to coincide with the 25th anniversary of the destruction of inner-city Plymouth in an air raid. The title of the programme and of this hymn was inspired by a photo caption showing the bombed parish church of St Andrew's where out of a heap of rubble in the nave a little apple tree had miraculously pushed its way through and stood in blossom.

Suggested tune: OLD 104TH

14 Celebration everywhere, any time 7.6.7.6. Trochaic

Christ is crucified today,
Christmas is tomorrow.
Lent will fall in summertime,
Easter is to follow.

Christ is here and everywhere,
one with all his people,
but we mark his whereabouts
with our Sunday steeples.

Christ – we often fence him out
from routine and Monday;
tie him down to holiness,
feasting, fasting, Sunday.

God, forgive our formal ways
and our special seasons;
free us from the faith that stills,
stifles or imprisons.

Make us whole, and bind in one
reason and emotion,
let our life-style manifest
day-to-day devotion.

Give us grace to seize and use
every situation,
any time for worship, love,
blessing, celebration!

Fred Kaan

Written for a Monday-morning staff worship service at the Geneva Ecumenical Centre, at the beginning of Lent 1973. While not wanting to disregard the 'special seasons' in the church's calendar, we also felt that there was a danger in over-emphasising them. I regret that at the time I had not yet come across Avery and Marsh's excellent 'Every morning is Easter morning from now on; every day's resurrection day, the past is over and gone ...'

Suggested tune: MELLING

15   An Easter song 9.8.9.8.D.

He's back in the land of the living,
the Man we decided to kill.
He's standing among us, forgiving
our guilt of the Good Friday hill.
He calls us to share in his rising,
to abandon the grave of our past;
he offers us present and future,
a world that is open and vast.

He's back in a world where the living
are robbing each other of joy,
where people for gain and destruction
the powers of nature employ.
From lofty respectable motives
are crosses erected today,
for people put people on trial
and evil is having its way.

But crosses are also the symbols
of life that is given and spent;
the signs of our hope and survival,
of Easter defeating our Lent.
Through people of passion, responding
to rise against hunger and hell,
new life shall arise from the ashes
of hatred, and all shall be well!

Fred Kaan

Not so much a hymn as a folksong about the Resurrection and its wider ramifications. I wrote it for the Pilgrim Church in Plymouth in 1965, and it was included in the 1972 full music edition of *Pilgrim Praise*.

Suggested tune: ST SULIEN

16   A hymn for Good Shepherd Sunday   7.6.7.6.7 7.

Jesus, Shepherd of our souls,
selfless in your caring,
lead us out to days of peace
and of thoughtful sharing.
Free our life from ill and war,
what is good in us restore.

Jesus, be our Shepherd still,
though the settings alter;
give us for our changing days
faith that will not falter.
Bless us in our modern scene
of computer and machine.

Christ, renew in us the charge
at your rising given:
that the Church in love should bring
to this earth your heaven.
Give us insight, show us how
life is here, the time is now.

May we with a shepherd's heart
love the people round us,
still recalling how your love
in our straying found us.
Point us to your caring ways,
guide us clearly all our days.

Fred Kaan

I wrote this especially for a BBC radio broadcast in 1965 when Good Shepherd Sunday (2nd after Easter) coincided with May Day/Labour Day. As with my paraphrase of Psalm 23, I have tried to bring the image of pastoral care into the context of our modern technological world.

Suggested tune: VARNDEAN

17   A hymn for Rogation Sunday   6.6.6.6.

Our God, we seek your face,
on you we must rely;
your never-measured grace
is ever standing by.

Give us your bread to eat,
sustain and make us whole
and with your wine complete
our joy of mind and soul.

To deep compassion move
the hearts of young and old;
grant on the seed of love
a harvest hundredfold.

New visions bring to birth,
compel us to be one;
stir up your Church on earth
for people to be won.

According to your will,
in Jesus' name we pray:
our deepest need fulfil,
our need of you today.

Fred Kaan

Written for Rogation Sunday (5th after Easter) for a united act of worship in the St Levan
Valley Group of Churches in Plymouth, of which the Pilgrim Church was a member.
Suggested tune: IBSTONE

18   A hymn for Ascension – quote, unquote   7.6.7.6.D.

Although our Lord has left us,
he leaves us not alone.
'Ascended into heaven',
he makes our earth his home.
Christ is alive and present
and makes us all akin;
in every human being
he walks the world again.

Christ brings, by his 'ascending',
God's love to all the earth,
a cosmic new dimension
to every human birth.
The candle is extinguished
and yet the light remains:
Christ who enlightens people
is in our midst and reigns.

Fred Kaan

In many Christian traditions the candle lit on Easter morning is extinguished on Ascension Day, after the Gospel reading in the service. The use of quotation marks in this text is quite deliberate – I believe that doctrinal and exegetical statements and claims ought more often to be put in inverted commas ...

Suggested tune: ST THEODULPH

3   Pentecost is Now

19 Wind of change

6.5.6.5.D.

Come, O Holy Spirit,
set the Church on fire;
strike it as the lightning
hits a posing spire.
Burn away the structures
and consume the sham
of our holy systems:
Come, in Jesus' name!

Blow away the cobwebs
of our stubborn past.
Come, send flying from us
myths unfit to last.
Wind of change, refresh us
and disturb our calm;
teach us what true love is,
take our hearts by storm.

Free us from the babble
of our Babel mind;
spark in us a language
all can understand.
Lighten then our darkness,
come and show us how
all the world lies open:
Pentecost is now!

Fred Kaan

I wrote this for a Pentecost celebration at the Ecumenical Centre in Geneva in 1972; it was first published in *Pilgrim Praise* later that year.
Suggested tune: AU CLAIR DE LA LUNE

4 The Church at Worship

Worship
Contrition
'Creed'
Baptism and Confirmation
Communion and Post-Communion
Belonging and Becoming
Close of Worship/Being Sent
Marriage
Thanksgiving
Church and Junior Church
Mothering Sunday and Father's Day
Church Dedication/Anniversary
Death and Dying/Remembering

20 A hymn on Sunday: three-fold anniversary

11.10.11.10.

This is the day when light was first created,
symbol and gift of order and design.
In light is God's intention clearly stated;
the break of day reveals his loving mind.

This is the day of our complete surprising,
repeat of Easter: Christ has come to life!
Now is the feast of love's revolt and rising
against the rule of hell and death and grief.

We join to praise, with every race and nation,
God who with humankind his Spirit shares;
strong wind of change and earth's illumination,
dispelling static thoughts and darkest fears.

This is the day of worship and of vision,
great birthday of the Church in every land.
Let Christians all confess their sad division
and seek the strength again as one to stand.

We pray that this, the day of re-creation,
may hallow all the week that is to come.
Inspire, O God, our daily celebration
of knowing, feeling earth to be our home.

Fred Kaan

Written for the Pilgrim Church in 1966, this is a bundling-together of the reasons we observe and celebrate Sunday: creation, the Resurrection and Pentecost.

Suggested tune: EASTWOOD or STRENGTH AND STAY

21 A hymn for ex-centrics*   8.7.8.7.D.

Peace be with all who worship here,
peace be to those who enter
this human-measured time and space
where Christ is at the centre:
a meeting place of 'heaven' and earth,
of freedom and tradition;
no longer strangers, we are one
in pilgrimage and mission.

God, who through self-disclosing love,
(in human form) befriends us,
creates the rhythm of the pulse
that brings us here – then sends us.
For Christians are not meant to stay
within these walls protected;
God wills the welfare of the *world*
and peace on *earth* reflected.

The call of Christ to serve in love
unsettles all who hear it
to venture out in faith and quest,
eccentric as the Spirit.
Now is the time to rise and go
– by bread and wine en-hearted –
to cross into the unexplored,
to risk a life uncharted.

Fred Kaan

*Greek: ex or ec = out, from
          kéntro = centre

Ex-centric/eccentric could be translated as: from the centre outwards

In many ways this is a 'prototype hymn', written in 1990; it gave rise to the hymn I later wrote
for the opening of the Uniting Church in Penrhys, Wales: 'God among us, Sense of life'
(No. 60). When I asked participants in a workshop I led at the 1995 San Diego conference of
the Hymn Society in the United States and Canada, which of the two texts I should retain,
they unanimously urged me to include *both* in any future book I might publish. So here they
are!

Suggested tune: ST GALL

22 'Today is the first day ...'

Each Sunday brings to mind again
that Jesus is risen: the Easter Sun!
And life has never been the same
since Easter came.

The sign of every rising sun,
the thought of the life in the grave begun,
renews our will to do and dare,
good news to bear.

Each Sunday sets the tone anew
for labour and leisure the whole week through,
for Easter turns the dullest day
to holy play.

Of all the days that still remain,
today is the first! Let us rise again
and run with haste to spread the word:
'We've seen the Lord!'

Each Sunday is the starting point
for freedom in which we are called to join
the movement that will lead to change
till love shall reign.

Fred Kaan

I wrote this during the Second Synod of the Church of North India in New Delhi in 1974. It was sparked off by a remark made by a delegate in a plenary session.

Suggested tune: LANNAMAN

LANNAMAN

Music Doreen Potter (1925–80)
Words Fred Kaan (1929–)

Each Sun - day brings_ to mind a - gain that

Je-sus is ri-sen: the Eas - ter Sun! And life has ne - ver

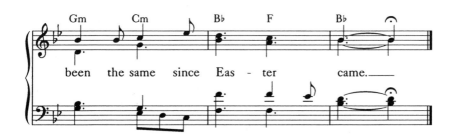

been the same since Eas - ter came.____

23   Come to your senses

If you have ears, then listen
to what the Spirit says
and give an open hearing
to wonder and surprise.

If you have eyes for seeing
the Word in human form,
then let your love be telling
and your compassion warm.

If you have buds for tasting
the apple of God's eye,
then go, enjoy creation
and people on the way.

If you have hands for caring,
then pray that you may know
the tender art of loving
our world of touch-and-go.

If you can smell the perfume
of life, the feast of earth,
then sow the seeds of laughter
and tend the shoots of mirth.

Come, people, to your senses
and celebrate the day,
for God gives wine for water,
the gift of light for grey.

Fred Kaan

I wrote this for Epiphany Sunday 1970, for an experimental worship service in the Calvin Auditorium in Geneva. The hymn is a plea for the use of all our senses in our exploration into God, and our living in the world. The biblical trigger is in the last verse – a loose reference to the wedding in Cana where Jesus changed the colourlessness of water into the sparkle of wine.

Suggested tune: CHERRY TREE CAROL

24   A hymn on worship and the arts   11.10.11.10.

We tingle with excitement at the knowledge
that God is love: the Easter-news is true!
We wait upon the prompting of the Spirit
in all the things our talents find to do.

With holiness and beauty on our palette,
we 'paint the town' in every hue of praise
and write our poetry of hope and longing,
with love and laughter decorate our days.

We raise the roof of cellar and cathedral
with sounds of jazz, with symphony and song,
and pray that in our practice and our playing
the consonance with heaven may be strong.

How can our hands be still, our feet be idle
through dance and music, colour and design,
invited by the One who comes, proclaiming
the Gloria of water into wine?

Let all the world weave tapestries of worship
to God, creation's origin and crown;
to Christ, the life and soul of Cana's party
and to the Spirit of the festive round.

Fred Kaan

I was one of five hymn-writers in the world who were invited by the American Lutheran Church to write a hymn to mark the 500th anniversary of Martin Luther's birth and baptism in 1483. The hymn was to express 'the joy of worship/witness as related to the arts'. It was premiered at a Festival of Worship and Witness in Minneapolis, USA, June 1983.

Suggested tune: INTERCESSOR

25   A hymn on music and praise 9 9.9 9.

Thank you, God, that long before all time
your great Spirit, source of reason, rhyme,
set the tone for all that came to be,
changed disorder into harmony.

Thank you for the prelude of your Word
– theme alluding to the final chord –
for the fugue of each creative deed,
for the score you give your world to read.

Thank you for the way creation sings,
for the beauty of the truth that rings,
for the keys in which we learn to play,
for the counterpoint of night and day.

Thank you, God, for melody and mirth,
for the hymns that circle all the earth.
Thank you for cantata, reggae, jazz,
songs of protest, symphonies of praise.

Thank you for a universe of sound,
for the lure of rhythm, dance and round.
Thank you for the life and lead of Christ:
Come, Lord Jesus, take us to the feast!

Fred Kaan

I was commissioned to write a hymn for Perrymount Methodist Church in Haywards
Heath, Sussex, England, to mark their choir anniversary in 1985, when I was the guest
preacher for the occasion.

Suggested tune: ETERNAL PRAISE

ETERNAL PRAISE

With a swing ♩ = 60

Music Carlton R Young (1926-)
Words Fred Kaan (1929-)

Thank you, God, that long be-fore all time your_ great
Spi - rit, source of rea - son, rhyme, set the tone for
all that came to be, changed dis - or - der in - to
har - mon - y.

Coda after stanza 5

slow arpeggio

26   A hymn for an international act of worship

Gathered here from many nations,
one in worship and intent,
let us for the days that greet us
all our hopes to God present,
    that our common life may be
    marked by trust, and truly free.

May the spring of all our actions
be, O God, your love, your Word;
make us conscious of your presence,
Spirit-filled, to sharing stirred.
    Help us, who your image bear,
    for the good of each to care.

Give us grace to match our calling,
faith to leave the past behind,
hope to grow into (y)our future,
love to shape the present time.
    Let the servant-mind of Christ
    in our lives be manifest.

Now ourselves anew committing
to each other and to you,
God, we ask that you will lead us
to the truth we need to do;
    that the world may soon become
    your great City of Shalom!

Fred Kaan

© 1974, 1996 Hope Publishing Company for USA and Canada and Stainer & Bell Ltd for all other territories

Written for international/ecumenical worship events, this hymn was first used at the 1972 meeting of the World Council of Churches' Central Committee in Utrecht, the Netherlands. I revised it in 1996. The hymn might also be useful in local and national contexts if the word *nations* were replaced by *churches*.

Suggested tune: NEANDER

27 A hymn for an international/ ecumenical worship event

11 11.11 11.

Divided by cultures, traditions and speech,
yet one in the Spirit, and caring for each,
we meet in response to the One who creates
our hope of reunion, who frees and unites.

Together, we look at our lives, and confess
our lack of compassion, our slowness to bless.
We pray for the will to re-plenish the earth
that life may be fair, free from hunger and dearth.

God's generous presence in human events
redeems us from shelters of selfish defence,
and gives us the courage – with others – to build
one home for the future: a gentle new world.

We come and we go with the Spirit that blows
and, following Jesus wherever he goes,
we rise against forces that torture and maim;
the peace that is God's we pursue and proclaim.

Fred Kaan

Following the 1975 Nairobi Assembly of the World Council of Churches, I was asked by the editor of the *International Review of Mission* to write a poem/song/hymn to capture the Nairobi experience. This truncated and slightly adapted text is here offered as a possible hymn for future international/ecumenical gatherings.

Suggested tune: ST DENIO

28   A hymn of contrition   7 7.7 6.

God, confronted with your might,
with your purity and light,
we are made with shame to see
all that we fail to be.

Conscious of our feeble will,
wanting good, but choosing ill,
we are sorry for our sin:
God, make us clean within.

Steady, God, our stumbling feet,
free our spirits from deceit.
Give us openness for pride:
we have no place to hide.

Lift us from despair and grief,
help us in our unbelief.
As we spread our hands to you,
fill us with life anew.

For the sake of Christ, forgive,
speak the Word, and we shall live.
Send us forward on our way,
God, with our heads held high.

Fred Kaan

Written for *Break Not the Circle*, the small collection of hymns published in 1975 for which
the Jamaican composer Doreen Potter (1925–80) composed all the tunes.
Suggested tune: DUNN'S RIVER

DUNN'S RIVER

Music Doreen Potter (1925–80)
Words Fred Kaan (1929–)

God, con-fron-ted with your might, with your pu - ri -

-ty and light, we are made with shame to— see—

all that we fail to be. heads held high.

29   A minimal hymn 7.7.7.7.5 5.

All that Christians have in life
is a story and a song;
bread and wine, a little faith
and a longing to belong.
    That is all they have,
    that is all they have.

All that Christians are in life:
they are people of 'the Way',
led by hunches, lured by hope,
now excited, then afraid.
    That is what they are,
    that is what they are.

All that Christians have and are
is a picture of their Lord,
is a signal and a glimpse,
is a gesture and a word.
    That is where they are,
    that is where they are.

Fred Kaan

During a seemingly endless and complex debate on constitutional reform at the 1976 Assembly of the Indonesian Council of Churches, a fellow ecumenical observer said to me: 'You know, when you take it down to the basics, all that Christians have in life is a piece of bread, a sip of wine and a song.' It inspired me to write this text there and then. Philip Potter, general secretary of the World Council of Churches, suggested the title of the hymn.

Suggested tune: CREDO

CREDO

Music Carlton R Young (1926–)
Words Fred Kaan (1929–)

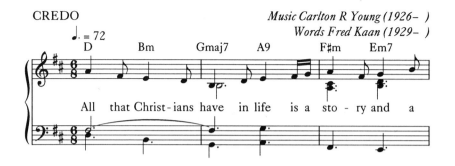

All that Christ-ians have in life is a sto - ry and a

song;___ bread and wine, a lit - tle faith and a

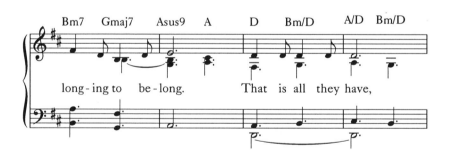

long - ing to be - long. That is all they have,

that is all they have. are.___

30   A hymn for the feast of baptism (1)   8.7.8.7.8 8.7.

Lord, come to us, share our delight,
    our marvel at creation,
as we in love and hope unite
    to pledge our dedication.
Christ, born on earth our life to live,
this child of loving now receive;
    bless all her* generation.

Be present, join us as we form
    a trusty circle round her,*
as we in church and world, at home
    with faith uphold, surround her.
Guide her in all that she* can be,
Lord, hold her fast, yet leave her free;
    let love release, astound her.

Lord, through the parents' open-ness,
    their caring inspiration,
teach her to treasure and embrace
    life with imagination.
Their home with peace and laughter bless
to make each day's togetherness
    a time of celebration.

Yes, Jesus, deepen our delight
    and heighten our affection
as now, in this baptismal rite,
    we feast the resurrection.
This tiny child: help her arise
(whatever still before her lies),
    and follow your direction.

Fred Kaan

*or: his, him, he

This hymn is a 'distillation' of two hymns I wrote for the baptism of my wife's grandsons in 1995 and 1997.
Suggested tune: LUTHER'S HYMN

31 A hymn for baptism (2)

Now in the name of Christ, who sent
to preach by word and sacrament,
upon this new-born child we pray
the strength of God in doubtful day.

Our names are written in God's hand,
who leads us to the promised land.
We rise in wonder from the flood
and love becomes our livelihood.

With Noah through disaster borne,
with Moses from the river drawn,
with Jonah from the sea released,
we celebrate this rising feast.

The water is a seal and sign
of costly love that makes us clean;
this love we see in Christ portrayed,
who rose triumphant from the dead.

We sing our thanks that old and young
so to the Church of Christ belong.
This is the covenant of grace;
we look salvation in the face.

Fred Kaan

In this hymn, written to try and supplement the rather small number of baptismal hymns in standard hymnbooks at the time, I have incorporated early Christian thoughts that draw lines to Old Testament traditions. Written for the Pilgrim Church in 1964.

Suggested tune: HERONGATE

32 A hymn for baptism (3)   8.7.8.7.D. including Chorus

LIVING WATER

♩ = 74

Music Carlton R Young (1926–)
Words Fred Kaan (1929–)

Out of deep, un - or - dered wa - ter God cre -

- a - ted land and life, world of bird and beast, and

la - ter two-some peo - ple, hus-band, wife. *There is*

wa - ter in the ri - ver bring- ing life to tree and

plant. *Let cre - a - tion praise its*

gi-ver: there is   wa-ter   in   the   font.

2   Wa-ter
3   Stand-ing

Out of deep, unordered water
God created land and life,
world of bird and beast, and later
two-some people, husband, wife.
There is water in the river
bringing life to tree and plant.
Let creation praise its giver:
there is water in the font.

Water on the human forehead,
birthmark of the love of God,
is the sign of death and rising;
through the sea there runs a road.
Chorus

Standing round the font reminds us
of the Hebrews' climb ashore.
Life is hallowed by the knowledge:
God has been this way before.
Chorus

Fred Kaan

I wrote this baptismal hymn for the Pilgrim Church in 1965, using a mixture of biblical
imagery. See for instance *Exodus* 14:22 and *1 Corinthians* 10:1–2.
Suggested tune: LIVING WATER

33 A hymn for baptism (4)

With grateful hearts our faith professing,
we ask you, God: come to our aid,
that we, our children re-'possessing',
may keep the vows that we have made.

We know that in your true providing
the young and old to Christ belong;
God, help us to be wise in guiding
and make us in example strong.

Give to all parents love and patience,
each home with Christian graces fill,
protect all children in temptations
and keep them safe in childhood's ill.

Accept, O God, our dedication
to fill with love the growing mind,
that in this church and congregation
the young a faith for life may find.

Fred Kaan

An early *Pilgrim Praise* hymn, written in 1964, to supplement the section of baptismal hymns in *Congregational Praise*. The idea of the last line came to me as a result of my involvement with Westward Television, Plymouth, for whom I regularly did late night epilogues, known under the title 'Faith for Life'.

Suggested tune: ST CLEMENT or LES COMMANDEMENS DE DIEU

34 A hymn for confirmation   CM

1a   O God, you called me by my name
when I had still no say;
today you call me to confirm
the vows my parents made.

1b   God, when I came into this life
you called me by my name;
today I come, commit myself,
responding to your claim.

You give me freedom to believe;
today I make my choice
and to the worship of the Church
I add my learning voice.

Within the circle of the faith,
as member of your cast,
I take my place with all the saints
of future, present, past.

In all the tensions of my life,
between my faith and doubt,
let your great Spirit give me hope,
sustain me, lead me out.

So help me in my unbelief
and let my life be true:
feet firmly planted on the earth,
my sights set high on you.

Fred Kaan

(Verse 1b is offered as an alternative where a person has not been baptised in infancy.)

I wrote this hymn in 1976 for my younger son Peter on the occasion of his confirmation in the National Protestant Church in Geneva, when I, unfortunately, was unable to be present as I was in Canada at the time for a tour of lectures and worship workshops. The hymn was not actually sung (the Geneva Church worships in French), but it was used at the confirmation of my daughter Alison (in the American Episcopal Church in Geneva in 1977), and of my elder son Martin (in the United Reformed Church in Hull, England, in 1978).

Suggested tune: UNIVERSITY

35   A Communion hymn

5.6.6.4.

As we break the bread
and taste the life of wine,
we bring to mind our Lord,
Man of all time.

Grain is sown to die;
it rises from the dead,
becomes through human toil
our daily bread.

Pass from hand to hand
the living love of Christ!
Machines and people raise
bread for this feast.

Jesus binds in one
our daily life and work;
he is of humankind
symbol and mark.

Having shared the bread
that died to rise again,
we rise to serve the world,
scattered as grain.

Fred Kaan

In this hymn I have tried to 'earth' the eucharistic understanding and experience by reminding worshippers that the bread does not appear mysteriously on our communion tables. Bread not only symbolises the process of being sown (dying) and rising, but it also represents people's daily work. I believe that when Jesus said 'I am the bread of life', he said much more than we expected. Verse 4 tries to make that point especially.

Suggested tune: MASSON

36 Hands shaped like a cradle

Put peace into each other's hands
and like a treasure hold it,
protect it like a candle-flame,
with tenderness enfold it.

Put peace into each other's hands
with loving expectation;
be gentle in your words and ways,
in touch with God's creation.

Put peace into each other's hands
like bread we break for sharing;
look people warmly in the eye:
our life is meant for caring.

As at communion, shape your hands
into a waiting cradle;
the gift of Christ receive, revere,
united round the table.

Put Christ into each other's hands,
he is love's deepest measure;
in love make peace, give peace a chance
and share it like a treasure.

Fred Kaan

© 1989 Hope Publishing Company for USA and Canada and Stainer & Bell Ltd for all other territories

---

This hymn was born when I watched people go forward to the altar rail to receive Communion: they shaped their hands like a cradle to receive the bread. (Bethlehem – house of bread – did not fully live up to its name until Jesus, the bread of life, was laid in the manger!)

The hymn was one of eight winning entries in the 1988 BBC TV Songs of Praise hymn-writing competition.

Suggested tune: ST COLUMBA

37　A hymn for after Holy Communion (1)　8 8 8.7.

God whose love is all around us,
who in Jesus sought and found us,
who to freedom new unbound us,
　keep our hearts with joy aflame.

For the sacramental breaking,
for the honour of partaking,
for your life, our lives re-making,
　young and old, we praise your name.

From the service of this table
lead us to a life more stable,
for our witness make us able;
　blessings on our work we claim.

Through our calling closely knitted,
daily to your praise committed,
for a life of service fitted,
　let us now your love proclaim.

Fred Kaan

Among the earlier hymns I wrote for the Pilgrim Church in Plymouth, there were several
related to the church's celebration of the sacraments – I felt at the time that there was a rather
serious shortage of Baptism and Communion hymns in the major hymnals.

Suggested tune: CHARING

38   A hymn for after Holy Communion (2)   LM

Now let us from this table rise
renewed in body, mind and soul;
with Christ we die and rise again,
his selfless love has made us whole.

With minds alert, upheld by grace,
to spread the Word in speech and deed,
we follow in the steps of Christ,
at one with all in hope and need.

To fill each human house with love,
it is the sacrament of care;
the work that Christ began to do
we humbly pledge ourselves to share.

Then grant us grace, Companion-God,
to choose again the pilgrim way
and help us to accept with joy
the challenge of tomorrow's day.

Fred Kaan

Another hymn written as a supplement to the existing Communion section in our hymnbooks in the mid-sixties. The words 'sacrament of care' (verse 3, line 2) were adopted as the theme for the 14th International Assembly of the World Federation of Diaconal Associations, held at Warwick University, England, in 1983. The hymn itself was used as the theme song of the Assembly.

Suggested tune: SOLOTHURN or NIAGARA

39   Communion Calypso

8 8.8 8.10.8.

Let us talents and tongues employ,
reaching out with a shout of joy:
bread is broken, the wine is poured,
Christ is spoken and seen and heard.
Jesus lives again, earth can breathe again,
pass the Word around: loaves abound!

Christ is able to make us one,
at the table he set the tone,
teaching people to live to bless,
love in word and in deed express.
Chorus

Jesus calls us in – sends us out
bearing fruit in a world of doubt,
gives us love to tell, bread to share:
God (Immanuel!) everywhere.
Chorus

Fred Kaan

In general, I suppose, a text comes into existence before a tune is found or composed for it, but this hymn is an exception. The Jamaican composer, Doreen Potter (1925–80) gave me her arrangement of a Jamaican folksong, which prompted me to write a *Communion Calypso* for it. It has become one of the most widely reproduced hymns Doreen and I wrote. It was first used in public at the 1975 Nairobi Assembly of the World Council of Churches.
Suggested tune: LINSTEAD

40   A hymn on not breaking the circle 10.11.10.11.

Break not the circle of enabling love
where people grow, forgiven and forgiving;
break not that circle – make it wider still,
till it includes, embraces all the living.

Come, wonder at this love that comes to life,
where words of freedom are with humour spoken
and people keep no score of wrong and guilt,
but *will* that human bonds remain unbroken.

Come, wonder at the One who came and comes
to teach the world the craft of hopeful craving
for peace and wholeness that will fill the earth:
Christ calls his people to creative living.

Join then the movement of the love that frees,
till people of whatever race or nation
will truly be themselves, stand on their feet,
see eye to eye with laughter and elation.

Fred Kaan

Of all the hymns I have written, this one was completed more quickly than any other – in 20 minutes. I wrote it while I was on holiday, too, which is very unusual in my 'scheme of things'. This text gave the title to a collection of new hymns *Break Not the Circle* (1975) for which all the tunes were composed by the Jamaican composer Doreen Potter (1925–80).

Suggested tune: LEYTONEN

41   Round-table church

7.6.7 7 7.6.

The church is like a table,
a table that is round.
It has no sides or corners,
no first or last, no honours;
here people are in one-ness
and love together bound.

The church is like a table
set in an open house;
no protocol for seating,
a symbol of inviting,
of sharing, drinking, eating;
an end to 'them' and 'us'.

The church is like a table,
a table for a feast
to celebrate the healing
of all excluded-feeling,
(while Christ is serving, kneeling,
a towel around his waist).

The church is like a table
where every head is crowned.
As guests of God created,
all are to each related;
the whole world is awaited
to make the circle round.

Fred Kaan

I wrote this text on the 7.40am train from Coventry to London on 14 December 1984. It owes its inspiration to a poem by Chuck Lathrop, a former missioner in the Appalachian Mountains.

Suggested tune: HOLLY LANE

HOLLY LANE

Music Pamela Ward (1946–)
Words Fred Kaan (1929–)

The church is like a ta - ble, a ta - ble that is

round. It has no sides or cor - ners, no

first or last, no ho - nours; here peo - ple are in

one - ness and love to - ge - ther bound.

42   A hymn on acceptance

7.6.7.6.D.

Help us accept each other
as Christ accepted us;
teach us as sister, brother,
each person to embrace.
Be present, Lord, among us
and bring us to believe:
we are *ourselves* accepted
and meant to love and live.

Teach us, O Lord, your lessons,
as in our daily life
we struggle to be human
and search for hope and faith.
Teach us to care for people,
for all – not just for some,
to love them as we find them
or as they may become.

Let your acceptance change us
so that we may be moved
in living situations
to do the truth in love;
to practise your acceptance
until we know by heart
the table of forgiveness
and laughter's healing art.

Lord, for today's encounters
with all who are in need,
who hunger for acceptance,
for justice and for bread,
we need new eyes for seeing,
new hands for holding on:
renew us with your Spirit;
Lord, free us, make us one!

Fred Kaan

This hymn was almost accidentally and at the last minute included in the 1974 edition of
Cantate Domino, when the editors were forced to drop a particular text for which the author
had asked an exorbitant fee, and my text happened to be of the right length to replace it. My
good friend and colleague Michael de Vries managed to do a German and Dutch translation
just before the printer's deadline.

Suggested tune: ACCEPTANCE

43 A hymn on becoming who we are   10.11.10.6 6.

You lead us, God, with miracle and grace;
we follow in your train of thought and calling.
With you we move in hope from place to place
and practise what shall be,
for you have set us free.

We give you thanks for all we've seen and heard,
but also for your future, never fearing
to stay within the earshot of your Word:
Word that divides, creates,
unsettles and unites.

Then make us of your beck and call aware,
help us accept the cost of 'kingdom-living',
the risk of our becoming who we are:
God, use our faith and doubt,
unite us, lead us out.

Fred Kaan

I wrote this hymn while attending the 1976 Assembly of the Indonesian Council of Churches in Salatiga, Java. Is there anyone in the world who feels inspired to compose a tune for it?

44   A hymn for the close of worship

6.6.6.6.8 8.

To show by touch and word
devotion to the earth,
to hold in high regard
all life that comes to birth,
we need, O God, the will to find
the good you had of old in mind.

Inspire our hearts to choose
the things that matter most,
to speak and do the truth,
creating peace and trust.
For every challenge that we face
we need your guidance and your grace.

Let love from day to day
be touchstone, guide and norm,
and let our lives portray
your Word in human form.
Now come with us, that we may have
your wits about us where we live.

Fred Kaan

First published in 1975 and revised in 1996, this hymn expresses one of my major preoccupations in life: how do we make a good transition from worship in church to representing Christ in the world. I often think that the most important 'liturgical movement' in worship is the opening of the church doors after the blessing. Now what ...? The tune for this hymn is by Ron Klusmeier of Canada, who has set more of my hymns to music than any other composer – well over 40 texts!

Suggested tune: LODWICK

LODWICK

Music Ron Klusmeier (1946-)
Words Fred Kaan (1929-)

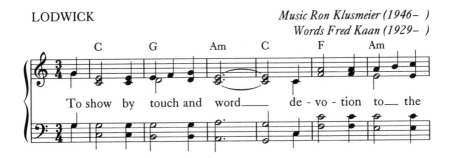

To show by touch and word____ de - vo - tion to__ the

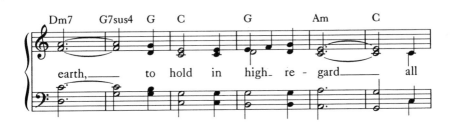

earth,____ to hold in high_ re - gard____ all

life that comes to birth,____ we need, O God,_ the

will to_ find the good you had_ of old in mind.

Reprinted by permission of the composer.

45   From worship to service

Lord, as we rise to leave this shell of worship,
called to the risk of unprotected living,
willing to be at one with all your people,
we ask for courage.

For all the strain with living interwoven,
for the demands each day will make upon us
and for the love we owe the modern city,
Lord, make us cheerful.

Give us an eye for openings to serve you;
make us alert when calm is interrupted,
ready and wise to use the unexpected:
sharpen our insight.

Lift from our life the blanket of convention,
give us the nerve to lose our life to others,
be with your Church in death and resurrection,
Lord of all ages!

Fred Kaan

This hymn, first introduced publicly at a 1973 'Come and Sing' event at Westminster Abbey, is focused on the need to make a meaningful transition from worship to service. The Swedish Mission Covenant Church chose it as the theme hymn for its 1998 General Assembly in Jönköping; the hymn has been for several years number one in the top-ten in the Swedish churches.

Suggested tune: LOBET DEN HERREN

46   On familiar ground

The fullness of the earth is God's alone
and life's unfolding is divinely known.
With humble hearts we recognise the claim
that every child and nation bears God's name.

To God belongs the scene of stack and tower,
as much as that of forest, field and flower;
God's love is focused on the city street
and on canteens where busy people meet.

On wards and sites, in workshops and in schools,
in work of mind and skilfulness with tools,
we feel God's presence in our daily round:
the place on which we stand is holy ground.

Then let us every given morning pray
that we may sanctify the city's day;
that Christ may guard our going out and in
and choose through us the world in love to win.

Fred Kaan

I wrote this for the Pilgrim Church in Plymouth in 1967, as a kind of 'supplement' or continuation of a sermon I had preached on the calling of Moses (*Exodus* 3): 'the place on which you are standing is holy ground.'

Suggested tune: CHILTON FOLIAT

47 A hymn on Abrahamic faith CM

O God of the eternal now,
why is your Church so slow
and lacks the will to venture out
where you would have us go?

If, Lord, it is our love of ease
by which we thwart your plan,
then stir us up, unsettle us
and lead us by the hand.

May we with courage take the risk
and leave the past behind,
to be a people on the move,
throw caution to the wind.

Give us the heart of Abraham,
for changes make us bold;
and bless us only so that we
in turn may bless the world.

Fred Kaan

Risk-taking has been called 'the second most important theme in the bible, following love'. 'God did not give us a spirit of timidity ...' (*2 Timothy* 7). I should like to see Abraham adopted as a kind of patron saint of adventurous Christians.

Suggested tune: ST STEPHEN (NEWINGTON)

48   A hymn on celebrating life   13.10.12.10.

Now let us translate in the language of human-ness
all we have heard with our ears and our tongue,
fully committed to beautiful holiness,
placed in a world where we gladly belong.

Appointed to spending a life of creativeness,
let us, with all who inhabit the globe,
worship the God who gives freedom for timidness,
feasting together on laughter and hope.

Let life be a song of devotion and cheerfulness,
let us embrace what is noble and good,
and in our love-making, friendships and tenderness
praise God who loves us in flesh and in blood.

Fred Kaan

Tom Harpur, religious editor of the *Toronto Star*, wrote in 1974 that this hymn 'scores what is undoubtedly a first in the history of Christian hymnody by calling on the singers to praise God in their love-making'. I wrote it for the 1972 edition of *Pilgrim Praise*, published by Stainer & Bell.

Suggested tune: WAS LEBET

O God who gave humanity its name,
in whom we live and move, from whom we came,
be with these two who now before you wait;
enlarge the love they come to consecrate.

May through their union other lives be blessed;
their door be wide to stranger and to guest,
give them the understanding that is kind,
grant them the blessing of an open mind.

Preserve their days from inwardness of heart,
to each the gift of truthfulness impart.
Their bond be strong against all strain and strife
amid the changes of this earthly life.

From stage to stage on life's unfolding way
bring to their mind the vows they make this day;
your Spirit be their guide in every move,
their faith in Christ the touchstone of their love.

God, bless us all to whom this day brings joy,
let no events our unity destroy,
and help us, till all sense of time is lost,
to live in love and not to count the cost.

Fred Kaan

What I have said about the dearth of hymns on baptism in the older hard-cover hymnbooks also applies to texts for marriage services. I wrote this in the mid-sixties.

Suggested tune: FFIGYSBREN

50 For a service of blessing of a marriage

8.4.8.4.8 8 8 4.

For this day of new beginnings,
thanks be to God;
for the hope that love is bringing,
thanks be to God.
> For the lure of life's horizons,
> for each vision that surprises,
> every challenge that arises,
> thanks be to God.

For each other, here assembled,
thanks be to God;
absent friends, in love remembered,
thanks be to God.
> For the worship that unites us
> and to acts of faith incites us,
> for the Gospel that delights us,
> thanks be to God.

For the calling of the Spirit,
thanks be to God;
for the 'yes' of all who hear it,
thanks be to God.
> For the blessing of receiving
> signs of healing and forgiving,
> practice in the art of living,
> thanks be to God.

For the peace we shall be sharing,
thanks be to God;
human vows of trust and daring,
thanks be to God.
> For this hour of celebration,
> partnership in dedication,
> for our place in God's creation,
> thanks be to God!

Fred Kaan

This is a very personal hymn, in that I wrote it for the Service of Blessing of the Marriage of Anthea Cooke and myself at Birmingham Cathedral in 1994. The service also included a hymn specially written for us by fellow hymn-writer Alan Gaunt.

Suggested tune: AR HYD Y NOS

51 A song to bride and bridegroom 11.10.11.10.D.

at a 'not quite religious' wedding ceremony

(Before the vows)

We form a circle (sign of celebration!)
to sing a song of friendship and support,
as we delight in all the loving choices
by which you to this festive point were brought.
You are the focus of our strong affection,
as now from heart to heart you make your vows,
accept each other freely, with devotion,
say 'yes' to all the joys that love allows.

(After the vows)

Our hearts are witness to your words of promise,
our eyes have seen you in your vows come home.
We bid you gladness in your new relating,
– as you are now or as you may become.
Be yours a life of learning, sharing, growing,
as husband, wife; but more! – as trusted friends,
and may your love enrich the lives of others;
on human loving peace on earth depends.

Go out in peace! And may with every rising
each day remind you of the vows you made.
Let faith in what is good in human nature
your words and deeds, your way of life pervade.
Go well! And may this day of new beginnings
be both for you and for us all a sun
to guide us on our path into the future;
true friendship be the bond that keeps us one.

Fred Kaan

I wrote this in 1997 for friends of my daughter's who have no religious affiliation but whose secular spirituality prompted them to ask me for a song which the wedding guests could sing with honesty. It was written with *Londonderry Air* in mind.

Suggested tune: LONDONDERRY AIR

52 A hymn for harvest thanksgiving 9.8.9.8. Anapaestic

Now join we, to praise the Creator,
our voices in worship and song;
we stand to recall with thanksgiving
that to God all seasons belong:

We thank you, O Source of all goodness,
for the joy and abundance of crops,
for food that is stored in our larders,
for all we can buy in the shops.

But also of need and starvation
we sing with concern and despair,
of skills that are used for destruction,
of land that is burnt and laid bare.

We cry for the plight of the hungry
while harvests are left on the field,
for orchards neglected and wasting,
for produce from markets withheld.

The song grows in depth and in wideness;
the earth and its people are one.
There can be no thanks without giving,
no words without deeds that are done.

Then teach us, O God of the harvest,
to be humble in all that we claim,
to share what we have with the nations,
to care for the world in your name.

Fred Kaan

One of the dangers inherent in harvest festivals is that they are so easily romanticised. Peter Cutts, one of today's foremost hymn composers, once hailed this text for its '... welcome recognition in a harvest hymn that abundance of crops is not universal'. Written for the Pilgrim Church in Plymouth, and first publicly introduced in the 1973 Westminster Abbey 'Come and Sing' series.

Suggested tune: HARVEST (Laycock)

53 The present tense

10.10 10. Dactylic

Thank you, O God, for the time that is now,
for all the newness your minutes allow,
make us alert with your presence of mind
to fears and longings that move humankind.

Thank you, O God, for the time that is past,
for all the values and thoughts that will last.
May we all stagnant tradition ignore,
leaving behind things that matter no more.

Thank you for hopes of the day that will come,
for all the change that will happen in time;
God, for the future our spirits prepare,
hallow our doubts and redeem us from fear.

Make us afraid of the thoughts that delay,
faithful in all the affairs of today;
keep us, Creator, from playing it safe,
thank you that now is the time of our life!

Fred Kaan

Written in 1967-ish for the Pilgrim Church in Plymouth, this hymn tries to spell out our priorities as far as our evaluation and use of time are concerned. One thing is for sure: tradition is dynamic rather than static; it means 'remembering forward'. We cannot hand Christ back, so to speak. Handing Christ on – tradition! – is future-orientated. Meanwhile, there is the here-and-now...

Suggested tune: QUEDLINBURG

54 A song for Palm Sunday and Easter

We have a king who rides a donkey,
and his name is Jesus:
Jesus the king is risen
early in the morning.

Trees are waving a royal welcome
for the king called Jesus:
Chorus

We have a king who cares for people,
and his name is Jesus:
Chorus

A loaf and a cup upon the table,
bread-and-wine is Jesus:
Chorus

We have a king with a bowl and towel,
servant-king is Jesus:
Chorus

What shall we do with our life this morning?
Give it up in service!
Chorus

Fred Kaan

I wrote this for an all-age Palm Sunday service at the Pilgrim Church in 1968. It is included in *Rejoice and Sing*, the 1991 hymnbook of the United Reformed Church, *not* at the initiative of its editorial committee, but as the result of a nationwide poll among Junior Church members – who voted overwhelmingly for the hymn's inclusion (to the dismay of one or two reviewers!) The choice of tune – *What shall we do with the drunken sailor* – has something to do with the disciples proclaiming the Resurrection on the day of Pentecost, and the crowds thinking they were drunk.

Suggested tune: DRUNKEN SAILOR

55 A back-to-front hymn
for the young in heart

7.6.7.6.

The language of the Hebrews
is right-to-left in print;
the end is the beginning,
their books are back to front.

The end is the beginning:
at Easter it began;
our life is topsy turvy,
for Jesus lives again.

Our life is topsy turvy,
the world is upside down.
The news that Christ is risen
has made us go to town.

The news that Christ is risen
has made the people's day!
We turn our hand to living;
the stone is rolled away.

Fred Kaan

I wrote this hymn for an all-age service on Easter Day in 1968, at the Pilgrim Church in
Plymouth. The title of the hymn describes what it tries to convey: Easter is the turning
upside down of all values. At the heart of the hymn is an allusion to *Acts* 17:6: 'These people
who have been turning the world upside down have come here also.' (And things have never
been the same since ...)

Suggested tune: ST ALPHEGE

56   The colourful year

When Noah's ark was high and dry,
there came a rainbow in the sky
and Noah heard a voice divine:
'I am your God and you are mine.'

This God who always faithful stays
has given colour to our days.
The shade with which the year begins
is purple: for the people's sins.

On Christmas day we see the light,
– the colour of the feast is white –
and when the Kings have left the scene,
our life runs into days of green.

With purple we return in Lent
to mourn for Jesus, emptied, spent.
'But sorrow is not meant to stay!'
proclaims the white of Easter day!

As red as flames of Pentecost,
so is the blood the martyrs lost.
Then, till the hopeful Advent sound,
we make with green the circle round.

The people of the church are led
through purple, white and green and red,
from fasting days to peaks of feast,
from dark of death to life in Christ.

Fred Kaan

I wrote this with the younger people at the Pilgrim Church in mind, after I had designed a set of pulpit and lectern hangings in the liturgical colours. The hymn is intended to teach children the sequences of the Christian year, and the colours that are used to symbolise the various seasons.

Suggested tune: TRURO

57 Four hymns for when younger people are about to 'leave' to go to their own groups or classes

A   6.6.6.6.

A house has different rooms,
we go through many doors;
the church is like a house
and all its space is ours.

The church is like a home,
a roof to shelter all:
together or apart,
from toddlers to the tall.

We're here in Jesus' name,
who said that he would be
among us in the crowd
or met as two or three.

Fred Kaan

Suggested tune: ST CECILIA

B   8.6.8.6.

Although we go our separate ways
to listen, learn and teach,
keep us together, God, and share
your love with all and each;

and let us hear the news of Christ
so that, when worship's done,
we may be full of Easter-life,
then go, and pass it on!

Fred Kaan

Suggested tune: ST BERNARD

C   7 7.7 7. Trochaic

All: Upstairs? Downstairs? God is there!
         God is here and everywhere.
         In the church and in the street,
         God is there for all to meet.

         Met in circles, large and small,
         we keep listening to God's call,
         keen in love and faith to grow,
         more of Christ-for-life to know.

Grown-ups: As you leave us, so we pray:
         'Peace be with you on your way.'
Children: 'Peace with you who stay behind,
         God be in your heart and mind.'

Fred Kaan

Suggested tune: UNIVERSITY COLLEGE

D   6.6.6.6.

         Before we came to church,
         God longed for us to come
         God's love invites us in,
         wants us to feel at home.

         Wherever we may be,
         our God has been before
         and Jesus is the key
         to open every door.

         Unite us, God, as now
         we go our 'separate' ways
         and let your Spirit guide
         each one who goes or stays.

Fred Kaan

Suggested tune: EDEN

I wrote these four short hymns during the course of 1987, while at Central (Ecumenical) Church in Swindon, England.

58   A hymn for Mothering Sunday

God of Eve and God of Mary,
God of love and mother-earth,
thank you for the ones who with us
shared their life and gave us birth.

As you came to earth in Jesus,
so you come to us today;
you are present in the caring
that prepares us for life's way.

Thank you that the Church, our Mother,
gives us bread and fills our cup,
and the comfort of the Spirit
warms our hearts and lifts us up.

Thank you for belonging, shelter,
bonds of friendship, ties of blood,
and for those who have no children,
yet are parents under God.

God of Eve and God of Mary,
Christ our brother, human Son,
Spirit, caring like a Mother,
take our love and make us one!

Fred Kaan

This was written in 1987 for Penhill United Reformed Church, the small Swindon housing estate congregation which I served as a part-time minister from 1985–89. The hymn was one of seven runners-up in that year's BBC TV hymn-writing competition, and was included in *New Songs of Praise 4*, published by Oxford University Press.

Suggested tune: SUSSEX

59 A hymn for Father's Day

God of Adam, God of Joseph,
God of sowing, soil and seed,
thank you for your world of promise,
milk and honey, wine and bread.

God, you make us your com-panions,*
sharers of your loving cup;
thank you for the generations,
weave of names and threads of hope.

May your passion for creation
be reflected in our own;
for our role in birth and nurture
make through us your presence known.

Thank you for all men entrusted
with the charge of fatherhood,
and for those who have no children,
yet are parents under God.

Abba (Father), God of Joseph,
human Christ whose name we bear,
Spirit, womb of life and wisdom,
thank you, God, for who we are!

Fred Kaan

* hyphenated on purpose: from Latin *cum* (together with) and *panis* (bread); people with
whom we share bread.

© 1994 Hope Publishing Company for USA and Canada and Stainer & Bell Ltd for all other territories

In 1989 the Gregorian Institute of America commissioned me to write a hymn for Father's
Day which would be a 'companion piece' running in close parallel to my 'Hymn for
Mothering Sunday' (see previous page). The two hymns were published in the 1994 Second
Edition of *Gather*, GIA's latest hymnal, both to the same tune, specially composed by
Thomas J Porter.

Suggested tune: SUSSEX

60   A hymn for the (re)dedication of a church, for a church anniversary, or simply for the 'opening-up' of Sunday worship

7.6.7.6.D.

God among us, Sense of life,
Christ whose love befriends us,
Spirit whose unsettling call
brings us here – then sends us,
bless this human-measured space
which in faith we enter;
God, in water, bread and wine,
be our source, our centre.

Show us how to be as one,
for each other caring,
of our lives to take control:
being, growing, sharing.
Let this be a hearth of peace,
quest and celebration;
God, we long to learn our role
in your good creation.

As we worship, wrestle, pray,
fire our hearts for mission;
what we have and who we are
bring to full fruition.
In our search for human worth
– where your children suffer –
use our vision, skills and hope
which in love we offer.

May tradition leave us free,
insights we inherit
make us doers of the Word,
challenge all who hear it.
Help us, God, in faith to rise,
by your love en-hearted,
cross into the unexplored,
risk a life uncharted!

Fred Kaan

© 1996 Hope Publishing Company for USA and Canada and Stainer & Bell Ltd for all other territories

I was commissioned to write a hymn for the opening of Llanfair Uniting Church, Penrhys, in South Wales in 1992, which brought together eight separate church traditions into one Local Ecumenical Project. Line 5 in verse 4 originally read: 'Help us, God of hill and well', which was a reference to the medieval Marian shrine and the ancient Celtic well which were both located in Penrhys, and which were important sites of pilgrimage prior to the Reformation. (See also No. 21.)

Suggested tune: AVE VIRGO VIRGINUM

61 A hymn for the dedication/ anniversary of a church

11.10.11.10.

We praise your name, O God of all creation,
for making plain the purpose of your will;
we thank you for creative inspiration
and our responding through design and skill.

We thank you that our faith has found expression
in walls that shelter those who worship here;
help us to be a house of intercession
and make us glad the world is always near.

We set this place apart for praise and preaching,
for breaking bread and practice to forgive;
we pray that through the open-ness of teaching
together, young and old, may learn to live.

Keep free our life from bondage of tradition
and let your Holy Spirit set the trend,
endow us with an urgent sense of mission;
our doors be wide to welcome and to send.

Your word be in our actions clearly spoken,
extend our church beyond the builder's plan
and use our witness as a vivid token
that you are still *with* woman, child and man.

Fred Kaan

This hymn was commissioned for the official opening of Derriford Congregational (now United Reformed) Church in Plymouth in 1967.

Suggested tune: ZU MEINEM HERRN

62   A hymn for a church anniversary   5.5.5.5.6.5.6.5. or
10 10.11 11.

We pause to give thanks
and focus our thought
on how far our God
his people has brought.
We pause for affirming
our 'yes' to his call,
pursuing his future:
life's fullness for all.

The future is here
as Christ sets us free;
we reach out in hope
for all that will be.
We go where God leads us
to time's furthest ends,
to share in life's mission
as partners and friends.

We rise and we risk
the course God has set,
to care for our world,
a world of 'not yet'.
At one in the Spirit,
we follow Christ's way
and put into practice
God's future today.

Fred Kaan

In 1987 the Council for World Mission, of which I was chairman at the time, celebrated its 10th anniversary in Hong Kong, and I was commissioned to write a hymn to mark the occasion. We sang it at the official thanksgiving service in English and in Cantonese (translated by Dr Hayward Wong). The hymn was also used in CWM member churches – 28 churches in 21 countries – on the Sunday following the Hong Kong celebration.

Suggested tune: HANOVER or LAUDATE DOMINUM

63   A hymn in the first person singular   10.11.10.11.

Today I live, but once shall come my death;
one day shall still my laughter and my crying,
bring to a halt my heart-beat and my breath:
O give me faith for living and for dying.

How I shall die, or when, I do not know,
nor where – for endless is the world's horizon;
but save me, God, from thoughts that lay me low,
from morbid fears that freeze my powers of reason.

When earthly life shall close, as close it must,
let Jesus be my brother and my merit.
Let me without regret recall the past
and then, into your hands commit my spirit.

Meanwhile I live and move and I am glad,
enjoy this life and all its interweaving;
each given day, as I take up the thread,
let love suggest my mode, my mood of living.

Fred Kaan

Rather than writing a hymn on death and dying (of which there are few – if any – in traditional hymnbooks), I decided to call this text 'A hymn in the first person singular'. After all, dying is an experience through which everyone of us has to pass individually. And so this hymn is a very personal statement, which I hope will not in any way come across as morbid or self-absorbed; after all: 'meanwhile I live ... enjoy this life'!

Suggested tune: HEARTBEAT

64   A hymn out of the depths

When, O God, our faith is tested
and our hope is undermined,
when our love of living shrivels
and we feel bereft and drained,
  then we turn to you and cry
  for your answer to our 'why?'

With emotions taut to breaking,
hearts with hurt and havoc frayed,
reason by remorse diminished,
souls distraught as if betrayed,
  God of bleakness and abyss,
  why have you forsaken us?

As we question and accuse you
out of depths of being tried,
could it be, God! that in weakness
you yourself are crucified?
  Are you with us in our grief?   .
  Help us in our unbelief!

Fred Kaan

This hymn arose out of my strong emotional involvement with a young couple who tragically lost their 15-months old son in a drowning accident in Dubai. It brought back to me the death of my own first-born son, and yet – having been through that experience – I had no glib words or easy answers for the parents; only my own rebelliousness to put alongside their distress. I did, however, manage to write this text which I was able to share with the mourners at the boy's funeral.

Suggested tune: FORTUNATUS NEW

65   A hymn for a funeral service

Lord of the living, in your name assembled,
we join to thank you for the life remembered.
Hold us, enfold us, to your children giving
   hope in believing.

Help us to treasure all that will remind us
of the enrichment in the days behind us.
Your love has set us in the generations,
   God of creation.

May we, whenever tempted to dejection
strongly recapture thoughts of resurrection.
You gave us Jesus to defeat our sadness
   with Easter gladness.

God, you can lift us from the grave of sorrow
into the presence of your own tomorrow;
give to your people for the day's affliction
   your benediction.

Fred Kaan

© 1968 Hope Publishing Company for USA and Canada and Stainer & Bell Ltd for all other territories

I wrote this text for the little *Pilgrim Praise* supplement (50 texts without music) which we put together at the Pilgrim Church in Plymouth in 1968.

Suggested tune: DIVA SERVATRIX

66   A hymn of grateful recall   8.6.8.6.D.
and renewed commitment

For all who have enriched our lives,
whom we have loved and known,
for saints alive among us still
by whom our faith is honed,
    we thank you, God, who came and comes
    through women, children, men,
    to share the highs and lows of life:
    God-for-us, now as then.

For all who with disarming love
have led us to explore
the risk of reasoning and doubt,
new realms not known before,
    we thank you, God, who came and comes
    to free us from our past,
    from ghettos of a rigid mind,
    from truths unfit to last.

For all whose laughter has unnerved
tradition gone awry,
who with incisive gentleness
pursue each human 'why?',
    we thank you, God, who came and comes
    to those who probe and ask,
    who seek to know the mind of Christ
    and take the church to task.

Now for each other and ourselves
we pray that, healed of fear,
we may re-live the love of Christ,
prepared in hope to err.
    Then leave us, God, who comes and goes,
    in human-ness to grow,
    to care for people, tend the earth,
    – the only earth we know!

Fred Kaan

I wrote this in 1993 for the memorial service of a good friend who had died of cancer, aged
56. Although the hymn is very personal in character in that it describes the kind of man he
was, it has already been widely taken up as a hymn suitable for thanksgiving and memorial
services, and for All Saints Day.

Suggested tune: KINGSFOLD or ELLACOMBE

God! As with silent hearts we bring to mind
how hate and war diminish humankind,
we pause – and seek in worship to increase
our knowledge of the things that make for peace.

Hallow our will as humbly we recall
the lives of those who gave and give their all.
We thank you, Lord, for women, children, men
who seek to serve in love, today as then.

Give us deep faith to comfort those who mourn,
high hope to share with all the newly born,
strong love in our pursuit of human worth:
'lest we forget' the future of this earth.

So, Prince of Peace, disarm our trust in power,
teach us to coax the plant of peace to flower.
May we, im-passioned by your living Word,
remember forward to a world restored.

Fred Kaan

I was commissioned by Coventry Cathedral to write a new text to replace the traditional Remembrance Day hymn, 'O valiant hearts', to be sung to Charles Harris's tune THE SUPREME SACRIFICE. The above hymn was first sung on Remembrance Sunday in 1989, when the service was broadcast nation-wide by Independent Television. The hymn is now also included in BBC *Songs of Praise* (OUP 1997).

Suggested tune: THE SUPREME SACRIFICE

5 Liturgy after the Liturgy

Reconciliation/New beginnings
Caring/Sharing/Stewardship
Peace and Justice
'Remembering forward'

When any person is to Christ united,
the past is gone, the present is re-stated.
How shall we live, to God's new world related?
Love will dictate it.

At peace with God, in love with those around us,
we are set free from all that cramped and bound us;
by love controlled, we give ourselves to others:
sisters and brothers.

In this new order, we are called to service,
sent in the strength of God whose nature love is,
proclaiming to the world by rhyme and reason:
Jesus is risen!

Fred Kaan

I wrote this hymn, based on *2 Corinthians*: 5, for the Uniting Assembly of the International Congregational Council (of which I was Minister-Secretary at the time) and the World Alliance of Reformed Churches, which took place in Nairobi, Kenya, 20–30 August, 1970).

Suggested tune: ROUEN

69 A hymn for people seeking release from broken relationships, and forgiveness for having failed others

8.7.8.7.

God! When human bonds are broken
and we lack the love or skill
to restore the hope of healing,
give us grace and make us still.

Through that stillness, with your Spirit
come into our world of stress,
for the sake of Christ forgiving
all the failures we confess.

You in us are bruised and broken:
hear us as we seek release
from the pain of earlier living;
set us free and grant us peace.

Send us, God of new beginnings,
humbly hopeful into life;
use us as a means of blessing:
make us stronger, give us faith.

Give us faith to be more faithful,
give us hope to be more true,
give us love to go on learning:
God! Encourage and renew!

Fred Kaan

This text, written in 1988, was triggered off (in part) by an experimental order of service compiled by URC minister John Johansen-Berg to help people who have been divorced but who 'desire to seek release from vows made before God so that they may feel free to make a new beginning'. I should like to think that the hymn may also be helpful in other circumstances where human relationships have broken down.

Suggested tune: LAUS DEO

God, how we long to be people more human
and to be part of a world more humane:
we want to be like the Jesus you gave us,
freed by his love and to service ordained.

God, let your Spirit reprove calm and caution,
all that is dull from our spirits remove;
fire our concern for the world and the nations,
send us to share with your children your love.

Yes, God, we long for your reign in our lifetime:
freedom from hunger and hatred and shame,
peace for all people and bread on each table;
save us from wasting the life of our time.

Fred Kaan

I wrote this especially for the 1972 full music edition of *Pilgrim Praise*.
Suggested tune: LIEBSTER IMMANUEL

71   The rape of the earth

God gave us as in trust to hold
creation and its wealth untold,
but we have with uncaring hand
destroyed its green and raped the land.

We strip the trees and leave them bare,
pollute the seas, the soil, the air,
and we have never truly faced
the outcome of our ways of waste.

But now, with millions underfed
and poison in our daily bread,
we view creation with alarm:
is there still time to heal the harm?

May God forgive the curse of greed,
alert our minds to human need,
that we again may purify
the life of earth and sea and sky.

Fred Kaan

This hymn sings of the way in which earth is plundered and human beings fail to re-plenish
it. *New Songs of Asian Cities*, published by the Christian Conference of Asia, and my own full
music edition of *Pilgrim Praise* both included this text in 1972.

Suggested tune: BRESLAU

For ourselves no longer living,
let us live for Christ alone;
of ourselves more strongly giving,
go as far as he has gone:
  one with God who chose to be
  one with us to set us free.

If we are to live for others,
share as equals human worth,
join the round of sisters, brothers,
that encircles all the earth:
  all the fullness earth affords,
  is the people's, is the Lord's.

Fighting fear and exploitation
is our daily common call;
finding selfhood, building nations,
sharing what we have with all.
  As the birds that soar in flight,
  let us rise towards the light.

Let us rise and join the forces
that combine to do God's will,
wisely using earth's resources,
human energy and skill.
  Let us *now*, by love released,
  celebrate the future's feast!

Fred Kaan

This was written for the 1974 Lusaka Assembly of the All Africa Conference of Churches. The theme of the Assembly, 'Living no longer for ourselves' was based on *2 Corinthians* 5:15.

Suggested tune: OTTAWA

73   A hymn on empty hands   11.10.11.10.

We come with empty hands, intent on sharing
our needs, our wealth – but more: all that we *are*.
We meet as partners for each other caring,
at one with people lacking voice or power.

We come to learn the courage of creating
a world of justice, hope and human worth,
to practise skills and secrets of translating
our words of faith into the life of earth.

We would be true in sharing of resources,
in freedom eager to receive and give,
be open to the Spirit's gifts and forces,
be broken for the world in which we live.

Then widen, God, our vision and vocation,
our joy in what in Christ you showed and gave;
as still you share your Self with all creation,
help us respond with all we are and have.

Fred Kaan

I was commissioned to write a conference hymn for the World Council of Churches consultation on Ecumenical Sharing of Resources in El Escorial, Spain, in 1987. The hymn may also be found appropriate during One World Week, observed in the UK in the third week of October (thus incorporating United Nations Day on the 24th).

Suggested tune: STRENGTH AND STAY

74   A hymn of creative love

Surrounded by a world of need,
by cries for healing, housing, bread,
our mind is given to despair
and hope is undermined by war.

Yet through the fabric of our time
there runs the liberating theme
of love that makes the world go round,
of love creative and profound.

This love is in the face of Christ,
in human life, made manifest;
its strong intent will conquer all,
it raises people when they fall.

Then help us, God, to understand
the claims and blessings of your plan
and use, to bring your reign about,
those in the Church and those without.

Fred Kaan

© 1968 Hope Publishing Company for USA and Canada and Stainer & Bell Ltd for all other territories

I wrote this in 1966 for the Pilgrim Church in Plymouth; it had its first more public airing in *New Church Praise*, a paperback supplement to the hard-cover hymnals that were in use in the two denominations (the Presbyterian Church of England and the Congregational Church in England and Wales) which merged in 1972 to become the United Reformed Church in England and Wales.

Suggested tune: BRESLAU

Choose life, choose love – the hour is late!
Say 'yes' to Christ and 'no' to fate.
Join hands with people of the faith,
reach out in hope to all who live.

In seeking space and life for each,
we need to practise what we preach,
to turn into creative deeds
the inner urges of our creeds.

With Christ-the-Least, renouncing power,
we face the challenge of this hour,
we rise against the death of earth,
the end of life, the end of birth.

The hour is late! Choose life, choose love,
with Christ into God's future move:
life to the full, the earth a feast,
through making, speaking, *being* peace!

Fred Kaan

In 1985 I was invited as a special guest to attend the All-Christian Peace Conference in Prague. The Conference theme, 'Choose life – the hour is late' triggered this text early on during the proceedings. We sang it later in a Conference session to EISENACH.

Suggested tune: EISENACH

76   A hymn on stewardship   7.6.7.6.D.

The earth, the sky, the oceans
and all that they contain,
the world with all its secrets,
they are our God's domain.
To rule this great creation,
God shares with humankind
his gifts of strength and courage
and an inventive mind.

To us from birth is given
our stewardship and brief:
to search for truth and purpose,
to find the heart of life.
God calls us to adventure
with work of hand and brain;
to share with all the people
the profits we may gain.

For quest and exploration,
our God has given the key
to free the hidden forces
and wealth of soil and sea.
To new advance in science,
research to conquer pain,
to growth in skill and knowledge
we are by God ordained.

We pledge ourselves to service,
that with the help of Christ
we may be faithful stewards
of all things that exist.
Whatever we discover,
on earth or out in space,
God grant that we may use it
to bless the human race.

Fred Kaan

I wrote this hymn for the 100th anniversary of the birth of the Antarctic explorer Robert
Falcon Scott (1868–1912), who was born and grew up in the Milehouse area of Plymouth
where the Pilgrim Church is located. The hymn was sung at a civic service at St
Bartholomew's Church – our neighbouring Anglican Church – whose priest-in-charge,
John Herklots, had commissioned the writing of this hymn.

Suggested tune: PEARSALL

77 A hymn on passionate peace-making 10 10.10 10.

God, while the world with war and hatred burns,
we skim across the surface of concerns
and though we pray for peace in Jesus' name,
we lack so often urgency and shame.

Forgive your Church its calm pursuit of peace,
from idleness of will our lives release;
for justice make us hungry, help us reach
with all our passion for the good of each.

Speak through our voice protesting at the skill
and science used to cripple and to kill.
Weep with our tears, as every weapon made
robs yet another child of human bread.

Cause anger to well up within our soul,
as all that you intended to be whole
and full of joy is trampled underfoot
by dint of war-machine and soldier's boot.

Teach us to use this anger and our will
to sweep away the forces out to kill
the life, the love you had of old in mind;
we pledge our word: we are *for* humankind!

Fred Kaan

This hymn came about after reading a poem entitled 'November 11' by Margaret Allen of
Glenridding, Cumbria. The poem was part of a larger hand-written collection of peace-texts
in an exercise book found after her death in 1985.

Suggested tune: WOODLANDS

78   The family of nations

We turn to you, O God of every nation,
giver of good and origin of life;
your love is at the heart of all creation,
your hurt is people's pain in war and death.

We turn to you that we may be forgiven
for crucifying Christ on earth again.
We know that we have never wholly striven
to share with all the promise of your reign.

Free every heart from haughty self-reliance,
our ways of thought inspire with simple grace;
break down among us barriers of defiance,
speak to the soul of all the human race.

On all who rise on earth for right relations,
we pray the light of love from hour to hour.
Grant wisdom to the leaders of the nations,
the gift of carefulness to those in power.

Teach us, good Lord, to serve the need of others,
help us to give and not to count the cost.
Unite us all to live as sisters, brothers,
defeat our Babel with your Pentecost!

Fred Kaan

Written for United Nations Day (24 October) in 1966. The hymn has been very widely reprinted, but it was not until the 1991 publication of the *Rejoice and Sing* hymnal by the United Reformed Church that the hymn appeared in a drastically revised version, using inclusive language. Two further changes are incorporated in the text as it appears here. Verse 3, line 1: *haughty* self-reliance replaces *pride and* self-reliance; and in verse 4, line 1: *rise* replaces *work*.

Suggested tune: INTERCESSOR

79 A hymn on life and peace

10 10.11 11.

We utter our cry: that peace may prevail,
that earth will survive and faith must not fail.
We pray with our life for the world in our care,
for people diminished by doubt and despair.

We cry from the fright of our daily scene
for strength to say 'no!' to all that is mean:
designs bearing chaos, extinction of life,
all energy wasted on weapons of death.

We lift up our hearts for children unborn:
give wisdom, O God, that we may hand on
– re-plenished and tended – this good planet earth,
preserving the future and wonder of birth.

Creator of life, come, share out, we pray
your Spirit on earth, revealing the Way
to leaders conferring round tables for peace,
that they may from bias and guile be released.

Be there with your Love, in protest and march
and help us to fire with passion your Church,
to match all our statements and lofty resolve
with being – unresting – in action involved.

Whatever the ill or pressure we face,
Lord, hearten and heal, give insight and grace
to think and make peace with each heartbeat and breath,
choose Christ before Caesar and life before death!

Fred Kaan

In 1983, when I was on holiday in Cuba, Olle Dahlén, Swedish ambassador to the United Nations, asked me to write a hymn for the Christian World Conference on Life and Peace in Uppsala, Sweden that year. The hymn was not only sung several times during the conference, but was also included in the official message sent out afterwards.

In 1985 this hymn was one of the eight winning entries in a BBC TV hymn-writing competition in the Songs of Praise Festival.

Suggested tune: HANOVER

80   A hymn on peace stewardship

You gave us, God, this earth to hold and cherish,
to praise you in our use of time and space,
but – blinded by our greed – the people perish;
we throw the gift of freedom in your face.

As with un-human madness we offend you
and with our bombs and bullets break your heart,
with money made from conflict we un-friend you,
we tear with prejudice your world apart.

We glorify the sin of pointless dying
through mines and missiles poised in soil and sea,
perfect the curse of daily crucifying
the Prince of Peace, each other, you and me.

Raise up among us prophets who will guide us
through action, speech and silence to your peace,
where fear, mistrust no longer will divide us,
where hurt is healed and captives are released.

Renew in us our faith and trust in Jesus,
the Man, the Woman in your image made,
and speak again your Word that truly frees us
to beat our sword into a simple spade.

Fred Kaan

© 1989 Hope Publishing Company for USA and Canada and Stainer & Bell Ltd for all other territories

I wrote this hymn for the 1986 Bread, not Bombs Week, an event organised annually by the
Campaign Against the Arms Trade.
Suggested tune: HARDING

81   Breaking the shackles of injustice   10.10.10.10.10.10.

Voice-over God, our Lover and Creator,
whose Word transformed disorder into peace,
who gave to all that is a name, a calling,
by whom all human wisdom was released,
God, give us confidence in living, loving,
the mind, the mood to make this life a feast.

Companion-Christ, in human terms among us,
let your redeeming, freeing presence teach
and help us not to measure those around us
by culture, race, by gender, creed or speech,
to look for that which is of God within them,
reach out, give thanks for what is good in each.

Ennobling Spirit, source of strength and passion,
inspire our hearts to hear the voiceless cry,
our will to break the shackles of injustice,
take down the barriers that demean, divide;
to give the hungry bread, the homeless shelter:
life in all fullness, that will *never* die.

Fred Kaan

I was commissioned to write a hymn for the 23rd Assembly of the World Alliance of Reformed Churches in Debrecen, Hungary, in 1997. The theme of the meeting was 'Break the chains of injustice' (*Isaiah* 58:6). The use of the term 'voice-over' owes its origin to the world of film, radio and television, where an unseen voice is sometimes used to hold the plot together – while the actors each have their own role to play. The first and final Word is often in a 'voice-over' mode!

Suggested tune: FINLANDIA

82 A hymn on human rights 8.7.8.7.8.7.

For the healing of the nations,
Lord, we pray with one accord,
for a just and equal sharing
of the things that earth affords.
To a life of love in action
help us rise and pledge our word.

Lead us forward into freedom,
from despair your world release,
that, redeemed from war and hatred,
all may come and go in peace.
Show us how through care and goodness
fear will die and hope increase.

All that kills abundant living,
let it from the earth be banned:
pride of status, race or schooling,
dogmas that obscure your plan.
In our common quest for justice
may we hallow life's brief span.

You, Creator-God, have written
your great name on humankind;
for our growing in your likeness
bring the life of Christ to mind;
that by our response and service
earth its destiny may find.

Fred Kaan

This is probably the most widely used hymn I have ever written. I wrote it to mark Human Rights Day (10 December) in 1965, at the Pilgrim Church in Plymouth. It has been sung at numerous national, international and state occasions around the world, among them the 25th anniversary of the United Nations, and the 50th anniversary of the International Labour Organisation in Geneva.

Suggested tune: GRAFTON

83 People matter, people count
8.7.8.7.D.

Sing we of the modern city,
scene alike of joy and stress;
sing we of its nameless people
in their urban wilderness.
Into endless rows of houses
life is set a million-fold,
life expressed in human beings
daily born and growing old.

In the city full of people,
world of speed and hectic days,
in the ever-changing setting
of the latest trend or craze,
Christ is present, and among us
in the crowd we see him stand.
In the bustle of the city
Jesus Christ is 'Everyman'.

God is not remote in heaven
but on earth to share our shame,
changing graph and mass and numbers
into persons with a name.
Christ has shown, beyond statistics,
human life with glory crowned,
by his timeless presence proving:
people matter, people count!

Fred Kaan

I confess that the main trigger for writing this hymn was my profound irritation with a hymn by Felix Adler (1851–1933): 'Sing we of the golden city pictured in the legends old; everlasting light shines o'er it, wondrous tales of it are told,' etc., etc. But what on earth (EARTH!) does this mean to a single teenage mum with a baby in a push-chair, living on the 14th floor of an apartment block where the lift isn't working? I thought I'd ask ... 'Everyman' is a reference to the 1529 English morality play, translated from the 15th-century Dutch original entitled 'Elkerlijc'.

Suggested tune: HYMN TO JOY

84   A hymn on daring to dream

10.10.10.10.

Rejoice in God who once upon a time
(before all time!) took love to shape a dream
and let it wake into the cosmic Word
that named the earth, with love as living theme.

Give thanks to Christ who calls us to be one
and shares our human-ness to show us how
to keep the dream alive, the vision clear:
a world at peace, the human race at play.

Pray that the Holy Spirit will pro(!)ceed,*
em-powering us to see Christ's mission through
and set the dream to song, en-act the Word,
put flesh on hope, make God's intent come true.

Let not, O God, the vision we have caught
fade as we rise, nor let it die away;
give us the faith with passion to pursue
that dream's fulfilment in the light of day.

Fred Kaan

* From the Nicene Creed: '... the Holy Spirit... who proceeds from the Father and the Son.'
The Latin 'procedere' has such a subtle variety of meanings – to go forward, advance, go on,
continue, turn out, make progress, succeed – all sounding rather future-orientated, and thus
meriting an exclamation mark, even in the middle of a word!

This is a revised version (written in 1998) of the hymn I was commissioned to write for the
bicentenary of the London Missionary Society/Council for World Mission in 1995. The
theme of the event was 'Dare to dream'. Copyright of the original text – first line: Sing high
to God, etc. – is controlled for the world except USA by the Council for World Mission,
32–34 Great Peter Street, London SW1P 2DB, UK.

Suggested tune: DARE TO DREAM

DARE TO DREAM

Music Maggie Hamilton (1953–)
Words Fred Kaan (1929–)

Re - joice in God who once up - on a time___

(organ)

— (be-fore all—time!) took love— to shape a— dream—

— and let it wake in - to the cos -mic Word___

— that named the earth, with love as liv -ing theme.

85 A hymn on not giving up 8.7.8.7.

Were the world to end tomorrow,
would we plant a tree today?
Would we till the soil of loving,
kneel to work and rise to pray?

Dare we try and give an answer,
reaching out in fragile hope,
touching lives with words of Easter,
break a loaf and share a cup?

Born into the brittle morning
of that final earthy day,
would we be intent on seeing
Christ in others on our way?

Pray that at the end of living,
of philosophies and creeds,
God will find the people busy
planting trees and sowing seeds.

Fred Kaan

Martin Luther was once asked how he would spend today if he knew that the world would come to an end tomorrow. He is reputed to have answered that he would plant an apple tree. I took this as the theme for an elders' conference I led in Solihull, near Birmingham, in 1980. It was not until 1986, though, that I wrote this hymn – and like No. 41, I wrote it on a 7.40am Coventry to London train.

Suggested tune: STUTTGART

6 Psalms – Freely

86   Psalm 8 – freely

God, how majestic is your name;
the earth and sky adore you,
the mouths of babies sing your praise
and children dance before you.

When I look up and see the stars
and think of space unending,
I marvel that you come and care
– us with your love befriending.

You lift us to the very height
of your creative likeness,
(just as you raised your Son from death
to Easter's wide-awake-ness).

Fred Kaan

This is one of several attempts to write free metric paraphrases of some of the Psalms. This one was included in the 1974 edition of *Cantate Domino*, the ecumenical hymnbook originally published under auspices of the World Student Christian Federation (from 1924 onwards), but subsequently 'taken over' by the World Council of Churches.

Suggested tune: WILFORD

87 Psalm 23 – freely

I can on God implicitly rely,
who stands in all events my person by.
It's God whose love into my prison breaks,
who leads me out and makes my soul relax.

Though I may go through nights of dark despair
and reach the very depth of thoughts that scare,
not even then will I give in to fear
for I am still convinced my God is near.

With all my heart I put my trust in God,
who wills for all his people what is good.
Wherever I may go, God too will come,
whose loving presence makes me feel at home.

Fred Kaan

© 1972 Hope Publishing Company for USA and Canada and Stainer & Bell Ltd for all other territories

As one who has lived in an urban context almost all his life, I tried my hand one day at writing a paraphrase of Psalm 23 avoiding its original rural imagery. Shepherds and flocks are pretty remote images for millions of people!

Suggested tune: CLIFF TOWN

88 Psalm 92 – freely

7.6.6.7.D.

How wide is life for living!
Come, people, raise your song
and let your praise be strong;
God's love is ours for giving.
Proclaim it in the morning,
declare it every night:
God's deeds can put to flight
our fears, our tears, our mourning.

The rich who thwart, oppose him
will not achieve their aim.
Our God will put his name
on those who love and choose him:
he will exalt the humble,
raise up the weak and poor,
and will make strong and sure
the feet of those who stumble.

Lift high your heads and flourish
like cedars rising up,
like palm-trees drawing sap
from streams that flow and nourish.
God is our strong salvation
in whom our lives rejoice
with instrument and voice
and daily celebration.

Fred Kaan

This free paraphrase of Psalm 92 was inspired by an even freer French version by Henri Künzler, who was the minister in Meyrin, Geneva from 1968–75. I wrote it with the tune in mind which originally appeared in the *Geneva Psalter* of 1562.

Suggested tune: MEYRIN

89   Psalm 130 – freely

Out of our failure to create
a world of love and care;
out of the depths of human life
we cry to God in prayer.

Out of the darkness of our time,
of days forever gone,
our souls are longing for the light
like watchers for the dawn.

Out of the depths we cry to God
whose mercy ends our night.
Our human hole-and-corner ways
by God are brought to light.

Hope in the Lord whose timeless love
gives laughter where we wept,
who every time, at every point
his word has given and kept.

Fred Kaan

This free paraphrase of Psalm 130 was written for the first 'home-spun' edition of *Pilgrim Praise* in 1967. Verse 3 draws on *John* 3:19–21.

Suggested tune: WALSALL

Out of our night of day,
darkness at noon,
we cry: God! Come and make
your presence known;
in Jesus come and help our shaky faith
and make us strong to face the pain of life.

Into our night of day
come with your light,
and let your Spirit break
the chains of fright.
Fulfil our hollow days that make no sense
and leave us not in life without defence.

Redeem our hearts for love,
free us from fear;
let crying in the night
make way for cheer.
So help us keep the promise you have made;
bring in the day when none shall be afraid.

Fred Kaan

This text will no doubt be recognised as being closely related to the theme of Psalm 130, but I can honestly say that the similarity is purely coincidental. American theologian and composer Carlton (Sam) Young wrote a moving tune for it, based on the motif of Bach's Cantata No. 38: *Aus tiefer Not schrei ich zu dir*. It was included in the 1980 *Choirbook for Saints and Singers*; this is the first time this tune is being published in the UK.

Suggested tune: DAYLIGHT

DAYLIGHT

Music Carlton R Young (1926–)
Words Fred Kaan (1929–)

♩ = 76–84

Out of our night of day, dark - ness at noon,
we cry: God! Come and make your pres - ence known;
in Je - sus come and help our shak - y faith
and make us strong to— face the pain of

1,2 life.
3 (Coda) -fraid.

7 Ten hymns from other lands

91 Almond blossom – sign of life 7.5.7.5.

Almond trees, renewed in bloom,
do they not proclaim
life returning year by year,
love that will remain?

Almond blossom, sign of life
in the face of pain,
raises hope in people's hearts:
spring has come again.

War destroys a thousand-fold,
hatred scars the earth,
but the day when almonds bloom
is a time of birth.

Friends, give thanks for almond blooms
swaying in the wind:
token that the gift of life
triumphs in the end.

Fred Kaan

At the 1983 Assembly of the World Council of Churches in Vancouver I was asked to translate a hymn by the Israeli poet and philosopher Schalom Ben-Chorin (and as it was urgently needed, I was given half-an-hour to do it! The above is the result). The text is based on Jeremiah 1:11–12, which contains a pun in the original text: almond branch and (God) watching sound very similar in Hebrew. The original title is *Freunde, daß der Mandelzweig (Das Zeichen)*.

Suggested tune: ST AIDAN

92 A hymn on being united in love

Bless, and keep us, God, in your love united,
from your family never separated.
You make all things new as we follow after;
whether tears or laughter, we belong to you.

Blessing shrivels up when your children hoard it;
move us then to share, for we can afford it:
blessing only grows in the act of sharing,
in a life of caring; love that heals and grows.

Fill your world with peace, such as you intended.
Teach us to prize the earth, love, re-plenish, tend it.
God, uplift, fulfil all who sow in sadness,
let them reap with gladness, by your kingdom thrilled.

You renew our life, changing tears to laughter;
we belong to you, so we follow after.
Bless and keep us, God, in your love united,
never separated from your living Word.

Fred Kaan

A translation of a text by the prominent contemporary German hymn-writer, Dieter Trautwein. The original was first sung at the 1979 Kirchentag in Nüremberg; I first introduced the English version at a Kaan Hymn Festival at the 1980 Princeton Conference of the Hymn Society in the United States and Canada. The hymn, for which Dr Trautwein also composed the tune, has become one of the most popular hymns in Europe, having been translated into at least ten languages.

Suggested tune: FRANKFURTER SEGENSLIED

93   Breaking bread with those in need 7.6.7.6.

Break your bread with those in need.
Bid your sisters, brothers,
who are homeless share your home,
and support each other.

With the hungry break your bread,
(you, too, first received it!)
Be with those who've lost all hope,
help them to retrieve it.

Christ who is the bread of life,
day by day Self-giving,
is among us and within,
source of life and living.

Jesus, Lord, we give you thanks
and your presence cherish.
Fill, inspire our here-and-now,
soul and body nourish.

Lord, we hunger for your bread,
feed us and enable
weak and strong to be at one
round your gracious table.

Fred Kaan

English text © 1999 Hope Publishing Company for USA and Canada and Stainer & Bell Ltd for all other territories. From the German original by Martin Jentzsch (1879–1967): 'Brich den Hungrigen dein Brot', © 1951 Merseburger Verlag, Kassel, Germany. Translated by permission.

I translated this from the German original by Martin Jentzsch (1879–1967), at the request of the Norwegian composer Knut Nystedt, who wanted to include this English version in a book of hymns for which he was composing all the tunes. What with Norway not yet a member of the European Union, a happy example of cross-border partnership!

Suggested tune: VENI, DOMINE

94 A hymn on Christ being alive

8.7.8.7.D.

Christ is risen, Christ is living,
dry your tears, be unafraid!
Death and darkness could not hold him,
nor the tomb in which he lay.
Do not look among the dead for
one who lives for evermore;
tell the world that Christ is risen,
make it known he goes before.

If the Lord had never risen,
we'd have nothing to believe.
But his promise can be trusted:
'You will live, because I live.'
As we share the death of Adam,
so in Christ we live again;
death has lost its sting and terror,
Christ is down to earth to reign.

Death has lost its old dominion,
let the world rejoice and shout!
Christ the first-born of the living,
gives us life and leads us out.
Let us thank our God who causes
hope to spring up from the ground;
Christ is risen, Christ is giving
life eternal, life profound.

Fred Kaan

The original text, 'Christo vive!' was written by the Argentinian poet Nicolas Martinez. This is one of several translations made for the 1974 edition of *Cantate Domino*, the international ecumenical hymnal.
Suggested tune: CENTRAL

95 God's kingdom among us

7.6.7.6.

God's kingdom is among us,
not vague and far away,
no fairy tale or fancy;
God's kingdom is today!

God meets us in the city,
in ambulance and fear,
in flashing light and siren
and in the surgeon's care.

God's kingdom is in churches,
at home and in hotels,
in hospitals and prisons
and at conveyor belts.

Then let us trace the kingdom;
its rule is never far:
God's kingdom simply happens
wherever people are!

Fred Kaan

Translation from the Swedish of a text by the famous poet Bo Setterlind. This translation, together with 19 others, was made for the Stainer & Bell collection *Songs and Hymns from Sweden* (1976).

Suggested tune: ST ALPHEGE

96   An Easter carol

6.7.6.7.D.

How many fruits we gain
by Jesus' dying proffered,
when he his life in pain
upon the tree had offered!
Yet would our gain be small
and vain his costly giving
if, after losing all,
Christ Jesus was not living.

Unsure would be our way
and dismal every morning,
were't not that every day
begins like Easter's dawning.
We are on earth at home,
redeemed from sin and crying,
for Jesus has become
the first-fruits from the dying.

How barren life would be,
how fruitless our devotion,
when all the guilt we feel
is deeper than the ocean!
How could the human race
endure this burden longer,
had not in evil's face
Christ proved to be the stronger?

The world of nature shows
that life must have an ending;
a nobler being grows
from death to life ascending.
This lesson can be read
in planting seed and sowing,
in grain that grows for bread:
praise God for all we owe him!

God's word invites and wakes
from death, through self-denial;
and by the hand God takes
us through defeat and trial.
Let every life be free
from all that would enslave it,
for risen again is Christ
who came to earth to save it.

Fred Kaan

In 1966 I decided to try and find the original Dutch text of the Easter carol 'This joyful Eastertide' to the tune VRU(E)CHTEN and attempt an English translation that stays close to the original. I found the 1684 text in the library of my old university, Utrecht.
Suggested tune: VRUECHTEN

97 The time will come

The day will come
when human dreams will reach fulfilment,
when this whole creation is to be redeemed
through justice, peace and joy.
Then shall the people with God walk hand in hand,
Then shall the people with God walk hand in hand.

The day will come
when nations will embrace each other,
when all shall be free and yet together bound,
safe in one earthly home.
Then shall the people with God walk hand in hand,
Then shall the people with God walk hand in hand.

The day will come
when earth will be renewed and flourish
through people who care for the Creator's gifts
of water, air and fire.
Then shall the people with God walk hand in hand,
Then shall the people with God walk hand in hand.

Fred Kaan

I was asked to translate into English a German text by Gerhard Schnath and Rudolf Otto Wiemer for the lively International Ecumenical Hymnbook *Thuma Mina* published in 1995 by the Basle Mission, Switzerland, and the Association of Protestant Churches and Missions in Germany.

Suggested tune: FUTURE TENSE

FUTURE TENSE

Music Carlton R Young (1926–)
Words Fred Kaan (1929–)

♩ = 110

The day will come when hu - man dreams will reach ful - fil - ment, when this whole cre - a - tion is to be re - deemed___ through jus - tice, peace and joy.

Then shall the peo - ple with God walk hand in hand,

Then shall the peo - ple with God walk hand in hand.

Our faults divide and hinder;
your grace can make us one.
We wonder at your rising,
your light is like the sun.
Unite us, God, in peace
and uphold us with your love.

You are our expectation
in loneliness and pain;
your healing and your pardon
are greater than our sin.
Chorus

O God, whose silent Spirit
enlightens and endows,
make us in faith receptive
and help us love your house.
Chorus

God, look upon the starving
and set the captive free;
share out among the people
the bread of unity.
Chorus

The cross will draw together
the round of humankind;
in Christ shall all the people
their true communion find.
Chorus

How happy are the people
who strive to be at one,
who live as sisters, brothers,
who lay their hatred down.
Chorus

Death can no longer hurt us,
triumphant is your Word.
Let life now grow and blossom,
O Jesus, risen Lord!
Chorus

Fred Kaan

I was commissioned to translate this original French text by Dominique Ombrie (who also composed the tune to go with it) for the 1974 edition of *Cantate Domino*.

Suggested tune: SEIGNEUR, RASSEMBLE NOUS

99 Worship and work must be one 11 11.12.7. and Refrain

Worship the Lord!
Praise the Creator, the Spirit, the Son,
raising our hands in devotion to God who is one!

Raising our hands as a sign of rejoicing,
and with our lips our togetherness voicing,
giving ourselves to a life of creativeness,
worship and work must be one.
Refrain

Praying and training that we be a blessing,
and by our gifts and skills daily confessing:
we are committed to serving humanity,
worship and work must be one.
Refrain

Called to be partners with God in creation,
honouring Christ as the Lord of the nation,
we must be ready for risk and for sacrifice,
worship and work must be one.
Refrain

Bringing the bread and the wine to the table,
asking that we may be led and enabled,
truly united to build new communities,
worship and work must be one.
Refrain

Now in response to the life you are giving,
help us, Creator, to offer our living,
seeking a just and a healing society,
worship and work must be one.
Refrain

Fred Kaan

This is a paraphrase of a Sinhalese (Sri Lankan) May Day Service Offering Hymn, which I wrote for *New Songs of Asian Cities*, a small paperback hymnbook published in 1972 by the Urban and Industrial Mission Committee of the Christian Conference of Asia. Serving as a translator and text consultant to the Jakarta Editorial Meeting of this Committee will remain in my memory as one of the most rewarding experiences of my life.

Suggested tune: WORSHIP THE LORD

100   Wide as the wind: God's love

11.10.11.10. and Chorus 11.10.

Your love, O God, is broad like beach and meadow,
wide as the wind, and an eternal home.
You leave us free to seek you or reject you,
you give us room to answer 'yes' or 'no'.
Your love, O God, is broad like beach and meadow,
wide as the wind, and an eternal home.

We long for freedom where our truest being
is given hope and courage to unfold.
We seek in freedom space and scope for dreaming,
and look for ground where trees and plants can grow.
Chorus

But there are walls that keep us all divided;
we fence each other in with hate and war.
Fear is the bricks-and-mortar of our prison,
our pride of self the prison coat we wear.
Chorus

O, judge us, God, and in your judgment free us,
and set our feet in freedom's open space;
take us as far as your compassion wanders
among the children of the human race.
Chorus

Fred Kaan

One of the finest contemporary hymns to have come out of Sweden, written by the doyen of Swedish hymn-writers, Anders Frostenson. I translated it for my collection *Songs and Hymns from Sweden*, published by Stainer & Bell in 1976.
Suggested tune: SOM STRANDEN

8 Magnificat for a New Millennium

Magnificat for a New Millennium

Come! Sing and live a world Magnificat,
the new Millennium with hope embrace.
Now is the time for trust and taking sides:
say 'yes' in love to all the human race.

Reach out in faith to what is still unknown,
each day a first day, every dawn a birth,
new ground for sowing seeds and planting trees,
'Lest we forget' the future of this earth.

Praise all that makes the world a better place:
creative thought, invention and design,
the anvil and the plough of making peace,
of sharing land and shelter, bread and wine.

Risk to become all we are meant to be,
live out tomorrow's destiny today!
Let us unite to keep the dream alive:
a world at peace, the human race at play.

As past and future in the present meet
and we take stock of where we were and are,
may Christ inspire and *be* our forward way,
and love with justice be our guiding star.

Fred Kaan

This is a very slightly amended version of the opening chorale of the cantata of the same name, which the Norwegian composer Knut Nystedt and I were commissioned to write for the opening of EXPO 2000, the world exhibition in Hanover in the year 2000. Knut Nystedt composed a tune for the above text especially for this book. A hymn without a number; a thousand years is a very long time by our clocks...

Suggested tune: WORLD MAGNIFICAT

WORLD MAGNIFICAT

Music Knut Nystedt (1915–)
Words Fred Kaan (1929–)

Come! Sing and live a world Mag - ni - fi - cat, the

new Mil-len - ni - um with hope em - brace. Now

is the time for trust and tak - ing sides: say

'yes' in love to all the hu - man race.

Index of First Lines

(First lines of choruses/refrains are shown in italics)

He's back in the land of the living *15*
How many fruits we gain *96*
How wide is life for living! *88*
I can on God implicity rely *87*
If you have ears, then listen *23*
In the beginning: God! *3*
Jesus lives again, earth can breathe again *39*
Jesus the king is risen *54*
Jesus, Shepherd of our souls *16*
Let us talents and tongues employ *39*
Lord, as we rise to leave this shell of worship *45*
Lord, come to us, share our delight *30*
Lord of the living, in your name assembled *65*
Mary, Mary, quite contrary *9*
Now in the name of Christ, who sent *31*
Now join we to praise the Creator *52*
Now let us from this table rise *38*
Now let us translate in the language of human-ness *48*
O God of the eternal now *47*
O God who gave humanity its name *49*
O God, you called me by my name *34*
Our faults divide and hinder *98*
Our God, we seek your face *17*
Out of deep, unordered water *32*
Out of our failure to create *89*
Out of our night of day *90*
Peace be with all who worship here *21*
Put peace into each other's hands *36*
Raising our hands as a sign of rejoicing *99*
Rejoice in God who once upon a time *84*
Sing we of the modern city *83*
Surrounded by a world of need *74*
Thank you, God, that long before all time *25*
Thank you, O God, for the time that is now *53*
The church is like a table *41*
The day will come *97*
The earth, the sky, the oceans *76*
The fullness of the earth is God's alone *46*
The language of the Hebrews *55*
Then shall the people with God walk hand in hand *97*
There is water in the river *32*
This is the day when light was first created *20*
Today I live, but once shall come my death *63*
Tomorrow Christ is coming *10*
To show by touch and word *44*
Unite us, God in peace *98*
Upstairs? Downstairs? God is there! *57C*
Voice-over God, our Lover and Creator *81*

We come uneasy, God, this festive season *12*
We come with empty hands, intent on sharing *73*
We form a circle (sign of celebration!) *51*
We have a king who rides a donkey *54*
We meet you, O Christ *13*
We pause to give thanks *62*
We praise your name, O God of all creation *61*
We tingle with excitement at the knowledge *24*
We turn to you, O God of every nation *78*
We utter our cry: that peace may prevail *79*
Were the world to end tomorrow *85*
When any person is to Christ united *68*
When Noah's ark was high and dry *56*
When, O God, our faith is tested *64*
With grateful hearts our faith professing *33*
Worship the Lord *99*
You gave us, God, this earth to hold and cherish *80*
You lead us, God, with miracle and grace *43*
Your love, O God, is broad like beach and meadow *100*
Your love, O God, is broad like beach and meadow *100*

Index of Titles

Index of Tunes

All the suggested tunes are available in United Kingdom, American and Canadian hymnbooks in common use. A number of these are listed in the Bibliography on page 143 for ease of reference. More specialist publications are also listed. Tunes printed in this anthology are marked with an *.

Index of Metres

Topical Index

The church is like *41*
We have a king *54*
We come with empty *73*

Celebration (see *Feast*)

Child, Children
Before all time *1*
Each year we sing *11*
For all who have *66*
God among us *60*
God! As with silent *67*
God, how majestic *86*
God, how we long *70*
God of Adam *59*
God of Eve *58*
God, while the world *77*
Lord, come to us *30*
Lord of the living *65*
Mary, Mary *9*
Now in the name *31*
The fullness *46*
Tomorrow Christ *10*
We praise your name *61*
We utter our cry *79*
With grateful hearts *33*
Your love, O God *100*

Church – its Community and Worship
A house has different *57A*
Although we go *57B*
Break not the circle *40*
Come, O Holy Spirit *19*
For this day *50*
God of Eve *58*
God whose love *37*
Help us accept *42*
O God, you called me *34*
Our faults divide *98*
Put peace *36*
The church is like *41*
Upstairs? *57C*
We praise your name *61*
With grateful hearts *33*

Church – its Unity
Although we go *57B*
Before we came *57D*

Break not the circle *40*
Come, O Holy Spirit *19*
For this day *50*
God among us *60*
God of Eve *58*
Help us accept *42*
Our faults divide *98*
Our God, we seek *17*
The church is like *41*
Upstairs? *57C*
We praise your name *61*
You lead us, God *43*

Church – its Outreach
Although we go *57B*
God among us *60*
God, while the world *77*
God whose love *37*
Jesus, Shepherd *16*
Let us talents *39*
Lord, as we rise *45*
Now let us from *38*
O God of the eternal now *47*
Peace be with all *21*
The fullness *46*
The language of *55*
To show by touch *44*
Upstairs? *57C*
We praise your name *61*
We utter our cry *79*

City
Each year we sing *11*
Gathered here *26*
God's kingdom *95*
Lord, as we rise *45*
The fullness *46*

Commitment
For this day *50*
O God, you called me *34*
We form a circle *51*

Creation (see *Earth*)

Earth
Although our Lord *18*
Before all time *1*

138

God is unique 6
God! When human bonds 69
God who spoke 4
In the beginning: God! 3
Our faults divide 98
Surrounded by a world 74
The church is like 41
We utter our cry 79
Worship the Lord 99

Word
As the glory 8
Bless, and keep us 92
Gathered here 26
God among us 60
God! As with silent 67
God is unique 6
God, while the world 77
If you have ears 23
In the beginning: God! 3
Let us talents 39
Mary, Mary 9
Now let us from 38
Rejoice in God 84
To show by touch 44
We come uneasy 12
You lead us, God 43

Work
As we break the bread 35
Each Sunday 22
God whose love 37
The earth, the sky 76

The fullness 46
Worship the Lord 99

World
Although our Lord 18
As we break the bread 35
Break not the circle 40
Come! Sing and live p. 126
Divided by cultures 27
For the healing 82
God! As with silent 67
God, how we long 70
God, while the world 77
He's back 15
Now join we 52
Now let us translate 48
O God of the eternal now 47
Out of our failure 89
Peace be with all 21
The church is like 41
Tomorrow Christ 10
We pause to give 62
Were the world 85
When any person 68
You gave us, God 80

Worship
Christ is crucified 14
Gathered here 26
Peace be with all 21
Thank you, God, that long 25
This is the day 20
We tingle 24

142

Bibliography and Acknowledgements

The publications named in the notes to the hymns, together with the main denominational hymnbooks in use in the UK, USA, Canada and Australia (to help with the location of tunes) are listed below:

100 Hymns of Hope (1992), Hope Publishing Company, Carol Stream, Illinois 60188, USA.

Australian Hymnbook (1979), HarperCollins Religious, 150 Jolimont Road, East Melbourne, VIC 3002, Australia.

The Baptist Hymnal/Christian Praise (1990), Broadman Press, 127 Ninth Avenue, N., Nashville, TN 37234, USA.

Baptist Praise and Worship (1991), Oxford University Press, Distribution Services, Saxon Way West, Corby, Northants NN18 9ES, England.

Book of Praise (1997), Presbyterian Church in Canada, 50 Wynford Drive, North York, Ontario, M3C 1J7, Canada.

Break Not the Circle (1975), Stainer & Bell Ltd, 23 Gruneisen Road, London N3 1DZ, England.

Broadcast Hymnbook, Oxford University Press, Distribution Services, Saxon Way West, Corby, Northants NN18 9ES, England.

Cantate Domino (1974), Oxford University Press, Distribution Services, Saxon Way West, Corby, Northants NN18 9ES, England.

Catholic Book of Worship III (1990), Canadian Conference of Catholic Bishops, 90 Paren Avenue, Ottawa, Ontario K1N 7B1, Canada.

Celebration Hymnal for Everyone (1994), McCrimmon Publishing Ltd, 10–12 High Street, Great Wakering, Southend-on-Sea, Essex SS3 0EQ, England.

Chalice Hymnal (1995), Chalice Press, PO Box 179, St Louis, MO 63166–0179, USA.

Congregational Praise (1951), United Reformed Church, 86 Tavistock Place, London WC1H 9RJ, England.

The Covenant Hymnal (1996), Covenant Publications, 5101 N. Francisco, Chicago, IL 60625, USA.

Ecumenical Praise (1977), Hope Publishing Company, Carol Stream, Illinois 60188, USA.

Gather Comprehensive (1994), GIA Publications, 7404 South Mason Avenue, Chicago, Illinois 60638, USA.

Hymnal Supplement (1984), Hope Publishing Company, Carol Stream, Illinois 60188, USA.

Hymnal Supplement (1991), GIA Publications, 7404 S. Mason Avenue, Chicago, IL 60638, USA.

Hymnal Supplement (1998), Concordia Publishing House, 3558 S. Jefferson Avenue, St Louis, MO 63118-3968, USA.

Hymnal: A Worship Book (1991), Brethren Press, 1451 Dundee Avenue, Elgin, IL 60120-1694, USA.

Hymns Ancient and Modern New Standard (1983), SCM/Canterbury Press, St Mary's Works, St Mary's Plain, Norwich NR3 3BH, England.

Hymns and Psalms (1983), Methodist Publishing House, 20 Ivatt Way, Peterborough PE3 7PG, England.

Hymns for Today's Church, Second Edition (1987), Hodder Headline plc, 338 Euston Road, London NW1 3BH, England.

Hymns Old and New, New Anglican Edition (1996), Kevin Mayhew Ltd, Buxhall, Stowmarket, Suffolk IP14 3DJ, England.

Hymns Old and New, Roman Catholic New Century Edition (1994), Kevin Mayhew Ltd, Buxhall, Stowmarket, Suffolk IP14 3DJ, England.

Magnificat for a New Millennium (Cantata), Norsk Musikforlag a/s, Box 1499 Vika, 0116 Oslo, Norway.

Moravian Book of Worship (1995), Moravian Church in America, 1021 Center Street, Bethlehem, PA 18016-1245, USA.

New Century Hymnal (1995), United Church Press, 700 Prospect Avenue, E., Cleveland, Ohio 44115–1100, USA.

New Church Praise (1975), Saint Andrew Press, 121 George Street, Edinburgh EH2 4YN, Scotland.

New English Hymnal (1986), SCM/Canterbury Press, St Mary's Works, St Mary's Plain, Norwich NR3 3BH, England.

New Hymnal for College and Schools (1991), Yale University Press, PO Box 209040, New Haven, CT 06520-9040, USA.

New Songs of Asian Cities, Christian Conference of Asia, Pak Tin Village, Mei Tin Road, NT, Hong Kong.

New Songs of Praise 4 (1989), Oxford University Press, Distribution Services, Saxon Way West, Corby, Northants NN18 9ES, England.

New Songs of Rejoicing (1994), Selah Publishing Co., 58 Pearl Street, Kingston, NY12401, USA.

Pilgrim Praise (1972), Stainer & Bell Ltd, 23 Gruneisen Road, London N3 1DZ, England.

Presbyterian Hymnal (1990), Westminster/John Knox Press, 100 Witherspoon Street, Louisville, KY 40202–1396, USA.

Psalter Hymnal (1987), CRC Publications, 2850 Kalamazoo Avenue, SE Grand Rapids, MI 49560, USA.

Rejoice and Sing (1991), Oxford University Press, Distribution Services, Saxon Way West, Corby, Northants NN18 9ES, England.

Ritual Songs (1996), GIA Publications, 7404 S. Mason Avenue, Chicago, IL 60638, USA.

Seventh-Day Adventist Church Hymnal (1984), Review & Herald Publishing, 55 W. Oak Ridge Drive, Hagerstown, MD 21740, USA.

Sing to the Lord (1993), Lillenas Publishing (Nazarene), Box 419527, Kansas City, MO 64141, USA.

Songs and Hymns from Sweden (1976), Stainer & Bell Ltd, 23 Gruneisen Road, London N3 1DZ, England.

Songs of Praise (BBC) (1997), Oxford University Press, Distribution Services, Saxon Way West, Corby, Northants NN18 9ES, England.

Supplement 96 (1996), Hope Publishing Company, Carol Stream, Illinois 60188, USA.

Supplement 99 (1999), Hope Publishing Company, Carol Stream, Illinois 60188, USA.

Thuma Mina (1995), Basileia Verlag, Basel, Switzerland and Strube Verlag, München–Berlin, Germany.

United Methodist Hymnal (1989), Abingdon Press, 201 Eighth Avenue S, PO Box 801, Nashville, Tennessee, TN 37202-0801, USA.

Voices United (1996), United Church of Canada Publishing House, 3250 Bloor Street West, Etobiocoke, Ontario, M8X 2Y4, Canada.

With One Voice (1995), Augsburg Fortress Publishers, PO Box 1209, Minneapolis, MN 55440, USA.

Worship III (1986), GIA Publications, 7404 S. Mason Avenue, Chicago, IL 60638, USA.

Worship Together (1995), The Christian Press, 159 Hendersen Highway, Winnipeg, Manitoba RL2 1L4, USA.

The Worshiping Church (1990), Hope Publishing Company, Carol Stream, Illinois 60188, USA.

The Author and Publishers gratefully acknowledge the assistance of the following in allowing reproduction of copyright material in the author's introduction and the notes to the hymns:

Caribbean Conference of Churches for the quotation from the text by Doreen Potter, *Look! Listen! Care!* (© 1981) (p.xv); Division of Christian Education of the National Council of the Churches of Christ in the USA for scripture quotations from the Revised Standard Version of the Bible (© 1946, 1952, 1971) and the New Revised Standard Version of the Bible (© 1989), All rights reserved; Hope Publishing Company for the quotation from the text by Avery and Marsh, *Every morning is Easter morning* (p.20); Hope Publishing Company and Oxford University Press for the quotation of two lines from the Erik Routley hymn *In praise of duty and delight* (p.xiii); University of Nebraska Press for the quotation from *Black Elk Speaks* by John G Neihardt, © 1932, 1959, 1972 by John G Neihardt, © 1961 by the John G Neihardt Trust (p.2); World Council of Churches for the quotation from *Risk: New Hymns for a New Day* (Albert van den Heuvel), WCC Publications, 1966 (p.xii).

If despite every care being taken, any copyright material is not acknowledged, the Publishers and Author apologise to those concerned and will correct the position in any future edition.

Further Reproduction of Texts and Tunes
The text of No. 91 is reproduced by permission of Hänssler-Verlag, Bismarckstraße 4, PO Box 1220, D–73765 Neuhausen, Germany.

The tunes CREDO (No. 29) and DAYLIGHT (No. 90) are administered in the UK by CopyCare, PO Box 77, Hailsham BN27 3EF.

The tune LODWICK (No. 44) is reprinted by permission of the composer, Ron Klusmeier, 880 Lakes Boulevard, Parksville, British Columbia, Canada V9P 2P8.

The tune WORLD MAGNIFICAT (p.127) is reprinted by permission of the composer, Knut Nystedt, 25b Vestbrynet, 1160 Oslo 11, Norway.

For all other texts and tunes, applicants in the United States of America and Canada should apply to Hope Publishing Company and applicants for the rest of the world to Stainer & Bell Ltd (see p.ii).